The Tokyo Trial Diaries of Mei Ju-ao

Mei Ju-ao

The Tokyo Trial Diaries of Mei Ju-ao

上海交通大學出版社
Shanghai Jiao Tong University Press

palgrave macmillan

Mei Ju-ao

ISBN 978-981-13-7794-5 ISBN 978-981-13-7795-2 (eBook)
https://doi.org/10.1007/978-981-13-7795-2

Jointly published with Shanghai Jiao Tong University Press
The print edition is not for sale in China Mainland. Customers from China Mainland please order the print book from: Shanghai Jiao Tong University Press.
ISBN of the China Mainland edition: 978-731-3150-80-6

Translation from the Chinese language edition: 东京审判亲历记 by Mei Ju-ao, © Shanghai Jiao Tong University Press, 2016. Published by SJTUP and Palgrave. All Rights Reserved.

This Palgrave Pivot imprint is published by the registered company Springer Nature Singapore Pte Ltd.
The registered company address is: 152 Beach Road, #21-01/04 Gateway East, Singapore 189721, Singapore

Editor's Note

This is the first English translation of the remainder of Dr. Mei Ju-ao's diary when he served as the Chinese judge in the International Military Tribunal for the Far East (the "Tokyo Trial"). Dr. Mei had the habit of keeping a diary. However, most of his diary entries were lost during the "Cultural Revolution." The following pages are but a small part of his diary, covering the period from his arrival in Tokyo to several days after the Tokyo Trial officially opened its sessions. Some pages of this part are also missing. This, of course, is far from reflecting the whole picture of the Tokyo Trial, but it helps us to grasp Dr. Mei's understanding of some important matters and his determination to strive for international justice, as well as his mindset as a jurist and a representative of China after its prolonged war of resistance against the Japanese invaders.

It is worth noting how the names are translated in this book. While the Japanese names are "Westernized" to show the given name preceding, all the Chinese names follow the Chinese custom of placing the family name before the given name. Also, we have adopted the current standard Chinese Pinyin system in terms of spelling, except for a few well-known "historical" names shown as they were or appearing in brackets in addition. Another phenomenon is that in the old days, a Chinese gentleman had a "courtesy name" apart from his official given name, often used among friends. The following "courtesy names" have appeared in Dr. Mei's diary, each followed by the person's official name here: Xiang Mingsi—Xiang Zhejun (Hsiang Che-chun), Wang Danru—Wang Zhi, Gu Yiqiao—Gu Yuxiu (Ku Yu-hsiu), Li Jizhi—Li Ji, Zhang

Fengju—Zhang Dinghuang, Zhang Boping—Zhang Qinglan, and Zhu Gongliang—Zhu Shiming. As for the names of places, we have used the spelling prevailing at the time of the Tokyo Trial so as to match its official records.

This book gives a vivid personal account of the establishment and early days of the International Military Tribunal for the Far East, and offers invaluable first-hand information and penetrating insight on the historical event of the Tokyo Trial.

Contents

About the Author

Mr. Mei Ju-ao was born in Nanchang, Jiangxi Province in 1904. He graduated from Tsinghua School (predecessor of Tsinghua University) in 1924 and then travelled to the United States to study at Stanford University and University of Chicago Law School, where he received his J.D. degree. After returning to China in 1929, Mr. Mei became a professor at Shanxi University, Nankai University, Wuhan University, Fudan University, and the Central Political School, successively or simultaneously, teaching courses including political science, civil law, criminal law, introduction to the common law, and international law. From 1934 onwards, he served as a member of the Legislative Council of the KMT government and had acted as acting chairman of its Foreign Affairs Committee. After the victory of the War of Resistance against Japan, he was assigned by the government, in 1946, to be the judge of the International Military Tribunal for the Far East representing China. During his nearly three years of trial work, he made great efforts to safeguard the national dignity and international justice, and contributed to the achievement of a just and fair trial. At the end of 1948, the KMT government appointed him as Councilor of the Executive Council and Minister of Justice, but he refused to assume office and fled to Hong Kong. He arrived in Beijing under the arrangement of the CPC representatives in early December 1949. From 1950 onwards, he served as adviser to the Ministry of Foreign Affairs, representative to the National People's Congress and member of its Bills Committee, member of the Chinese People's Political Consultative Conference, member of the World Peace Council, Executive Director of the Chinese People's Institute of Foreign Affairs, and Director of the Chinese Society of Political Science and Law. Mr. Mei suffered injustice in the "Anti-Rightist Movement" and the "Cultural Revolution." He passed away in Beijing in 1973, at the age of 68.

List of Figures

The Tokyo Trial Diaries of Mei Ju-ao

Abstract This pivot considers the process and the impact of the International Military Tribunal for the Far East, otherwise known as the Tokyo Trial, which was convened in 1946 to try political and military leaders of Japan accused of involvement in war crimes. It gives a vivid personal account of the establishment and early days of the International Military Tribunal for the Far East. Written from the perspective of a Chinese judge who was both jurist and witness, this unique text offers invaluable first-hand information and penetrating insight on the historical event of the Tokyo Trial.

Keywords The Tokyo Trial and World War Two · International Military Tribunal for the Far East · Second World War and Japan · War Criminals in Japan · International War Crimes Jurisdiction · International Politics and War Crimes · Participants in the Tokyo Trial

March 20, 1946, Wednesday

It was a fine day today. When I pushed the window open on the tenth floor of Cathay Mansion, there was a red shining sun in the azure sky, a scene that I had not seen for three weeks now. It has been five weeks since I left Chungking for Shanghai. In the first two weeks, the sun

Mei Ju-ao, *The Tokyo Trial Diaries of Mei Ju-ao*,
https://doi.org/10.1007/978-981-13-7795-2_1

shone warmly every day as if it were mid-spring. However, the following three weeks were full of raindrops lingering without stop, almost making me forget how the sun ever shed its light.

To avoid the discomfort of walking in the rain in early morning, I applied to the headquarters of US army for a room in Cathay Mansion, one of Shanghai's skyscrapers located in the old French Concession, a Western-styled structure called "the 13-storied building" by locals. The Mansion was used as Japan's military command when Shanghai was under the Japanese control. After Japan's surrender, the US army took it over and set it as a dormitory for the US military officers and a guest house. The Air Transport Command (A.T.C.) is located on the first floor. Any passenger who is to fly to Japan or the US by a military airplane must arrive here by 7:00 a.m., go through some procedures, and then take the Command's bus for the Jiangwan Airfield.

Though a skyscraper in Shanghai, Cathy Mansion had become a water dungeon due to the 20ish-day raining. Only through the long boards laid in front of its gate and in the back hall could people walk in and out of the Mansion. When I moved in last night, this mess caused me a big trouble.

Strange enough, the rain stopped overnight and the water surrounding the Mansion receded. Looking outside of the window, the sun rose from the east against the blue sky, almost a mid-spring day and totally different from yesterday's dismaying cloud and fog. This change, though made by the hand of Mother Nature, did delight and excite me quite a lot.

Last night, I talked for a long time with some friends, especially with Xiang Mingsi [Xiang Zhejun, or as Hsiang Che-chun] who came back from Japan recently. Thinking that the process of my flying would start right from this hotel and there should be no worry for being late, I went to bed too late, and it was already 7 o'clock when I woke up.

After a hasty washing, I had no time for breakfast and immediately rushed to find a porter to carry my luggage downstairs, when it was no earlier than 7:30. Quickly going through the procedures, all the passengers were invited upstairs to watch a film clip entitled *Passenger Notice* which showed us how to wear a life jacket, and how to protect and save ourselves in case of a plane accident. This clip went on for about fifteen minutes with thorough and intelligible details. The Americans' respect for life and their serious and scientific approaches were manifest in these arrangements.

Afterwards, we walked downstairs, and the staff took a roll-call for us to get on the bus one by one. Since my name was titled with "Judge," he called me first, which aroused the interest of those American officers. In the eyes of Westerners, especially in the UK and the US, judges are of the most respectable profession. In a country where the rule of law is strictly observed and laws have supremacy, judges are naturally honored and dignified.

However, they were curious about this Chinese judge: where did he come from and why was he heading for Tokyo?

Silence prevailed. The bus was fast, driving through the crowded streets one after another. An officer saw a piece of luggage with my name card hanging on it. He tried to look calm, but meanwhile revealed an expression of pride like a detective having found a clue. I knew he wanted to read that card, so I turned my head toward the window while catching a glimpse of his move. When I turned back, his face changed, as if he was telling his companions that he had found a secret. He then showed more respect to me, because, in his mind, a judge to be sitting in an international military tribunal set up by the Supreme Commander for the Allied Powers (SCAP for short, or the General Headquarters—GHQ) was a most honorable person. We exchanged a few words of courtesy and, when getting off the bus at Jiangwan, he helped me with my luggage and accompanied me to embark the airplane, showing great friendliness to me.

The plane took off at 9:30 a.m. With my stomach empty and without even a sip of tea, I felt a little uncomfortable but there was no choice for me. Before the take-off, a crew member asked us to put on our life jackets; then fifteen minutes after we were off the ground, he told us to take them off, saying that the danger was over. We were all somewhat confused.

The plane was a medium transport aircraft which could take forty or fifty passengers. But in this plane, there were only about a dozen, less than one-third of its load. Apart from two Japanese and me, the rest were US military officers, some going to Tokyo and others to the US via Tokyo.

That young officer was sitting next to me. We had become acquaintances by now and chatted quite a lot on various topics. Meanwhile, I was no longer thirsty as he served me a cup of tea every thirty minutes. His name was McLeod. He told me that he had studied law for one year after graduating from college, which he would like to continue after his military service was completed. In the army, he started as an ordinary soldier and was promoted to a lieutenant after several years in the battlefield. From this one example, we can see how fair the US military system is and what a high level of education the American servicemen have.

Speaking of the two Japanese passengers, I wondered what kind of people they were, but I never asked them any question, although they were humble and polite and looked like trying to talk with me. This was for two reasons. First, the US military officers seemed to disgust or ignore them, or at least acted coldly toward them, which made me feel inconvenient to contact them despite my curiosity. Secondly, even if I asked them, they might not be able to answer me in Chinese or English while I had no knowledge of Japanese. But I was boggled by the idea that they were likely to be peaceniks or communists, like Kazuo Aoyama and Wataru Kaji, otherwise they would not be entitled to travel in a US military airplane without any form of supervision (if they were prisoners, they would be escorted by armed soldiers). This riddle about who they are still lingers in my mind.

Amid chatting with McLeod, I sometimes looked out of the window, at the vast and endless sea or the crystal blue sky. Time passed by quickly. Soon we came over Japan and would land at Atsugi Airport in fifteen minutes. The crew member instructed us to put on our life jackets and then take them off again, and the plane landed in two minutes. This flight was very smooth and comfortable, and the weather was pleasant, too. It was 4:00 p.m. when we arrived. I felt lucky—lucky for a man who had been suffering from the rain for three weeks in Shanghai.

Upon landing, when I was about to shake hands with McLeod and say goodbye, suddenly an officer in a colonel uniform rushed in and asked loudly for "Judge Wei." I guessed he was the guy sent to pick me up and I told him that I was Judge Mei, not Wei. He said yes, he was here to pick me up but had confused Mei with Wei. He added that the US headquarters in Shanghai sent a telegram to the GHQ, which assigned him to meet me at the airport. The rank of colonel is pretty high in the US army, and his words further surprised the passengers—What kind of judge is he? Why does he come to Tokyo? And why is he welcomed so greatly?

The officer was Colonel Huff, a director of protocol or director of hospitality under Douglas MacArthur. He has followed General MacArthur for many years. Having gone through numerous tough battles as a veteran, he has nevertheless been given such a menial job as receiving and sending off guests now.

With Huff's care, everything seemed fine. I followed him to get off the plane, and set my foot on Japan's soil. His guard and driver carried my luggage, with all the procedures exempted. It took no more than several minutes for us to drive out of the airport and head for Tokyo, which is 42 miles away from Atsugi. The ride of over one hour also took me through the outskirts of Yokohama, thus enabling me to see the ruins of both Yokohama and Tokyo left by the aerial bombings.

A curiosity seized me. Looking at the scenes along the road and the men and women passing by, I poured out questions to Colonel Huff, like *The Analects* says: "When Confucius entered the Ancestral Temple, he asked about everything."

Huff has a gift of the gab and is familiar with the situation, so he answered my questions to my satisfaction.

I cannot write down everything I saw during the drive, neither do I remember all the questions I asked Huff. My general impression was that all the factories in Yokohama and Tokyo were bombarded and burned. Only then, I came to realize what was meant by "scorching a city."

Huff's family lived in Manila and his house was burned by the Japanese. He pointed to a square with piles of debris and rubble, saying that he was pleased to see it. I told him that my home was also burned down when the Japanese army occupied Nanking, so I could definitely share his feelings.

The men and women that I saw on the road had different facial expressions. Most men walked slowly with their heads down, and looked like having heavy thoughts in their mind; most women, by contrast, walked briskly with a smiling face and an air of indifference. However, whether men or women, they are no longer what I saw in Japan twenty-two years ago. Who have brought about such changes? The war criminals that we are about to try must be held responsible for it. They disrupted the world order, caused great damage to China, and also ruined the future of their own nation. How dangerous it was for a country to be run, not by statesmen but by a bunch of unscrupulous military men with neither political mind nor global vision! An ever promising nation has been doomed, as the saying goes, "You reap what you have sown." It is a tragedy in human history, and also an important lesson.

My thoughts and feelings are bountiful as today is my first day to step on the soil of Japan, home of the enemies whom we fought against for eight years. But my observations are prone to be superficial, so I will stop here. Since I will stay here for at least four or five months, I will have time to observe more, and then make more solid conclusions.

At about 5 o'clock (it was already 6 o'clock in Tokyo, one hour ahead of Shanghai), we arrived at the Imperial Hotel, a world-renowned guesthouse.

The Imperial Hotel used to be where the GHQ was located, and Douglas MacArthur stayed here for some time. In my imagination, this hotel should be a towering mansion, prominent with its Western features, at least comparable with the Park Hotel or the Cathay Mansion in Shanghai. However, the fact contravenes my imagination. The Imperial Hotel is an antique two-story "house," with no magnificent appearance. For all the modern equipment one may need, it does not look fashionable or majestic. It is said that this hotel's biggest advantage is its earthquake-resistant structure. In 1923, the Great Kantō Earthquake hit Tokyo and shook almost everything down, but this hotel still stood firm. Before the recent War, it was used by the Japanese government to accommodate foreign guests, and now all the important GHQ officials of or above the rank of brigadier general reportedly live here.

Upon arrival, Colonel Huff called Lt. Morris, manager of the hotel, to accompany us to Room 288, which had been designated for me. "This room has been waiting for you for nearly a month," said Morris with a smile. "It has been reserved for you since we were informed of your arrival in Shanghai."

The room is located in the very east end of the second floor. It is quite spacious, with three separate parts: a living room, a bedroom and a bathroom, as well as a big balcony (which can hold two traditional Chinese banquet tables) and a small balcony. The ventilation is good. From the balconies, I can see the streets and a square below. Inside the rooms, all the utensils I may need have been provided. After two months' hustle and bustle, I am very pleased to settle down in such a quiet environment.

I chatted with Huff and Morris for about ten minutes, and it suddenly occurred to me that I had to meet our Chinese delegates and the judges from other countries who had arrived earlier.

Morris went to make telephone calls for me. To my disappointment, Gen. Wang Danru [Wang Zhi], China's general liaison officer, and Dr. Gu Yiqiao [Gu Yuxiu, or as Ku Yu-hsiu], who is visiting Japan, have gone to Nagasaki to see the atomic bombing ruins; Sir William Webb, the Australian judge, has returned home for business, while the judges from the UK, the US, Canada, the Netherlands, and New Zealand are touring together around Kyoto since they have been in Tokyo for quite some time with nothing to do right now. All of them may come back in two or three days.

I remembered Mr. Liu Zenghua from China's Ministry of Foreign Affairs and Mr. Tang, our deputy liaison officer in Tokyo. Morris instantly connected me with them over the telephone, and I invited them for a chat in the evening.

Being tired after the journey, I asked the hotel attendant to serve dinner in my room. Then Messrs. Liu and Tang along with a Mr. Dai came. We chatted for about an hour, when they asked me what was happening in China, and I asked them about Tokyo, until it was 9:00 p.m. before we realized it.

After they left, I unpacked my luggage in haste and took a hot bath before going to bed.

March 21, 1946, Thursday

It was already 8 o'clock when I woke up. Being too tired and sleepy last night, I forgot to turn off the light and adjust the gas stove, but still slept tight for about ten hours, which I cannot do in ordinary days.

I felt it unnecessary to go out, considering that the other judges went to Kyoto, that my old schoolmates Gen. Wang and Dr. Gu were also away, and that I already met with Messrs. Liu and Tang last night. I should take a good rest in the hotel today.

I had breakfast, lunch and supper all in my room. The food here is in American cuisine, supplied by the GHQ, and the ingredients are said to be shipped from the US. All the related costs are considered part of the occupation fee, which is to be paid by the Japanese government.

While the quality was not bad, the dishes were somewhat monotonous, with all the officials stationed in Tokyo taking the same meals without any choice. I read the two newspapers provided by the GHQ for free: *Stars and Stripes* and *Nippon Times*, published by the GHQ and the Japanese respectively.

After breakfast, I put my luggage in order and looked around from my balconies. Soon Morris came. We greeted each other, then he asked me if I wanted to have my room rearranged. He also told me that the GHQ had designated a sedan car for my use, with a military driver named Wallace. I told him that I did not need the car today but he should come tomorrow morning.

Today's weather was as good as yesterday's, but I did not walk out of my room. All the things were completed with the help of the hotel attendants.

Speaking of the Japanese attendants, whether male or female, they are all polite and deferential, showing their courtesy in an extreme manner. Whatever they are asked to do, they will take all the orders, say yes in a low voice, and bow to recede with a smile. However, what their true feelings are, what they think of Japan's fiasco and of the Chinese people, these are behind their smiles, of which I have no idea.

After supper, I recalled that I had to write home. But who can help me take the letters to China? Anger and shame filled my heart when I realized that, after more than six months of the occupation of Japan, there is still no official correspondence channel with China. Even the Chinese officials stationed here cannot send letters to their families in China. What a pity!

I have kept the habit of playing Tai-Chi every day for two years, but I did not do it in the past three days. Recalling this at night, I practiced one set. Then I took a hot bath and went to bed at 10 o'clock.

March 22, 1946, Friday

The weather was even better than that of yesterday. Pushing the windows open upon waking up, I saw no cloud in the sky. The sun shed its light all over the balcony, extending its warmth to the carpet inside. The spring may have really arrived at last.

But the people I wanted to meet with are not yet back. To go out touring the city? I do not have a guide, and my secretary Luo Jiyi, a "Japan hand," failed to come along with me as he is still stranded in Hong Kong. It seemed that I would miss out such a delightful day again. Determined, since there was not much choice for me, I dismissed the driver at 9 o'clock. I spent the whole day in the hotel and had only room-served meals.

I dragged a chair near the balcony, and spent several hours reading a book, which was given to me as a gift by Mr. Chen Tingrui who had just returned to Shanghai from the US. The book, *War Criminals: Their Prosecution and Punishment* by Sheldon Glueck, a Harvard professor of criminal law and criminology, is a masterpiece and has come at a much opportune time for me, for which I should thank Mr. Chen. Back in Shanghai, my restless mind and too many social activities had prevented me from making a serious study, where I read only a few dozens of pages. But today, in the peaceful surroundings and with a tranquil mind, I of course seized this good opportunity to read as much as possible.

While reading in the sunshine, I from time to time took a look from the balcony at the Japanese men and women and the American soldiers passing by on the streets down there. It seemed to me that there was little contact between American soldiers and Japanese people, and they seldom walked side by side with each other. There was neither hostility nor friendliness and amicability between the two groups, but rather, they were indifferent as if they had not seen each other. These observations were made merely on the surface, subject to possible changes later.

What I found peculiar today was that the Japanese people, both men and women, looked physically strong, especially the young women who were stout with glowing faces. Such a finding seems somewhat contrary to the foreign newspaper reports that the Japanese people are leading a hard life, suffering from scarcity in food supply, insufficient rationing, and strict restrictions on cash withdrawal from the bank (it is said that each Japanese can only withdraw 100 yen per day, equaling US$ 6.6 at the official exchange rate of 15 yen per dollar, which becomes 30 to 80 yen per dollar in the black money market). Should the news reports be true, how could the Japanese look so healthy and dress themselves in fine clothes—at least much better than ordinary Chinese people. This myth has lingered in my mind and I will try to find the truth. There must be something hidden underneath. Alas, perhaps they are spreading falsified news again!

I received a telephone call in the evening, from Justice E. Stuart McDougall, the judge representing Canada in the Tokyo Tribunal who stays downstairs at Room 188 right under my room. He told me that among the five judges who went to Kyoto, he and the American judge came back this evening, while the rest would return tomorrow night. He was eager to meet me, and I expressed welcome. In less than five minutes, he came upstairs. McDougall is a veteran judge specialized in criminal cases at the court of Montreal, Canada. Though 62 years of age, he does not look old; neither does he like his age to be mentioned—he really has a young heart. He talked to me with a sincere attitude, a broad smile and a good sense of humor. He told me that Sir William F. Webb had gone back to Australia for business after long waiting in Tokyo. It was said that Webb's back was hurt and he might not be back soon; in this case, Gen. MacArthur designated Justice Erima Harvey Northcroft, the judge from New Zealand, to act as President of the Tribunal for the time being. Northcroft has also been in Tokyo for almost two months. There are seven judges now with me included and, according to the Charter of the Tribunal, the number of the judges here—seven out of nine—have met the requirement for a quorum. However, said McDougall, we'd better take unified actions in international affairs. He did not believe that we would have much accomplished before the arrival of the judges from France and the Soviet Union, especially the latter. The judges who came earlier held a few meetings, which were mainly conversational except for some deliberations on the draft Rules of Procedure proposed by Webb. He said that, having nothing to do, they felt a little bit bored these days.

Hearing this, I felt happy and worried at the same time. On one hand, I am glad that I am not a late bird and will be able to join the drafting of the various court rules as well as the discussions and decisions on all the issues before the Tribunal opens its sessions; on the other hand, it seems to me that the time for us to really start working is unforeseeable and unpredictable. However, I am still lucky as compared to those who have been idle here for one or two months. McDougall and I talked for about half an hour before he left my room. It was very kind of him to invite me to visit the Tribunal's courthouse together tomorrow morning.

Alas, finally I met one of my colleagues today and learned about the recent situation of the Tribunal. What a relief! After writing in my diary and playing a set of Tai-Chi, I went to bed just after 10 o'clock.

March 23, 1946, Saturday

Having finished washing and breakfast, I called McDougall to tell him that I would come to his room. After a short chat, we set out for the courthouse by his car. My car also followed, so that my driver would know the route next time.

The Tribunal is located in the former Japanese Ministry of War building, about a 10-minute drive and not too close to the hotel. The Ministry of War (i.e., the Ministry of the Army), also known as *Junbu* (actually a combination of the Ministry of War, the Ministry of Navy, the Army General Staff and the Navy General Staff) was the birthplace of Japan's aggressive war policies and the headquarters for the major war criminals (warlords). MacArthur's approval for the selection of this place as the site of an international tribunal to try war criminals may contain a profound meaning and convey a particular message.

The War Ministry's former domicile is spectacular, and the walls surrounding it look forbidding. The building, though not gorgeous, displays power and grandeur. Its interior and exterior structure has not been affected by the bombings.

We went upstairs and, led by McDougall, I visited all around: the conference room, the President's office (formerly Hideki Tojo's) and the judges' offices. Each judge is provided with two rooms, one for himself and the other for his personal secretary. All the offices are large, exquisitely furnished with carpets, curtains, desks and chairs, as well as wall paintings, and are full of sunlight. It will really be pleasant to work here. My office is to the left of the conference room, between the British and the Canadian judges'. All our offices have door plates showing "The Honorable Mr. Justice XX." We can see that judges are truly respected in the Anglo-American culture, for a judge's name is always preceded with a title, like "Honorable Mr. Justice" or at least "Judge."

The Tribunal's security arrangements are exceptionally tight, with guards both in and outside of the building. Meanwhile, every judge's office has a NO ENTRANCE sign; a visitor can only walk in through the office of the judge's secretary. Also, the canteen, the cafe and the bar are restricted with a sign "STAFF ONLY," and even the washrooms have a sign "OCCUPATION FORCE ONLY. NO ADMITTANCE FOR JAPANESE."

Finally, I came to the courtroom of the Tribunal with McDougall. It has been transformed from the auditorium of the War Ministry and is still under renovation. I saw dozens of Japanese craftsmen working there. The courtroom is truly mighty and magnificent, no wonder Mr. Keenan told me when he was in Shanghai, "No other court in the world is comparable with the Tribunal's courtroom except for the American Supreme Court."

Then, McDougall took me to the office of Justice John P. Higgins, the American judge. Higgins is said to be 52 or 53, but his gray hair makes him look like at least 60 years old. He was once a US Congressman with a good political reputation, but in the recent dozen years, he has been engaged in judicial practices serving as the chief justice of the Massachusetts Superior Court. Massachusetts is one of the American states that have the best judicial system and nurture the greatest number of judges. The Higgins Court has 32 full-time judges, a startling number as to the court's size in the US. It is said that it was Mr. Keenan who asked MacArthur for the appointment of Higgins to represent the US in Tokyo. Justice Higgins kept talking about his court during our conversation.

Saying good-bye to Higgins, McDougall and I came back to our hotel.

After lunch, I, like yesterday, took a nap and read Glueck's book until McDougall invited me to have dinner together in the canteen, where there is a table reserved for the judges and serviced by thoughtful waiters and waitresses. This arrangement is very convenient for us, as otherwise we may be at a loss as to where to go in such a big canteen.

After dinner, the three of us sat and chatted in the corridor. Higgins was most sincere and open to any topic. He said that he admired China, especially the bravery of the Chinese people: to fight to the last drop of blood and never to surrender. He regarded China and the US as brothers, and such brotherhood would only thrive and never fade. He also told me that the love and admiration of China was common among ordinary Americans. "I represent the 130 million people, not just myself."

This was the first time that I had heard such a forthright and expansive remark in quite a few years.

March 29, 1946, Friday

The weather turned fine again today. When opening the newspapers upon getting up, I found another article written by Owen Lattimore reprinted in *Nippon Times.* Mr. Lattimore is a famous political commentator and an expert in Far East affairs, who once served as a political adviser to Mr. Chiang Kai-shek. He is now one of the US representatives in the Japan war compensation commission, and has recently visited Japan and China.

The theme of his article is to warn the US that, if not properly controlled, Japan will rise again as an industrial and economic power and will manipulate and rule the Far East region, making it impossible for China, Korea, the Philippines and other countries still weak in industrial development to emerge and join the competition. He believes that Japan is feigning poverty and hardship; in effect, there is no food scarcity as otherwise its people would not be able to keep so healthy and strong, in much better conditions than the people in Shanghai, Peking or Korea. This is the same as what I have observed in the past week or so. Lattimore says that, by virtue of Japan's solid foundation in industrial technology and with the possibility of obtaining raw materials, it will not only revive, but can also take a dominant role in the Far East and place China in an extremely disadvantaged position. What's more, says he, Japan should not be dealt with solely from the American perspective or stance, but the interests of those economically backward countries in the Far East should be taken into consideration. Therefore, he proposes that the Allied Powers ban the export of industrial raw materials to Japan, and encourage Japan's land reform which will gradually turn its farming tenants into land-holding farmers, increase agricultural production, and make Japan self-sufficient. His article hits the nail on the head, and I totally agree with it. We should make a loud appeal so that the Allied policy over the governance of Japan will not deviate from the right direction, to avoid making another major mistake in history.

When I was reading before noon, a telephone call from downstairs told me that Dr. Gu and Gen. Wang had come back from Kyoto. They came to my room and shared with me a lot about their trip, which stirred my yearning for that city. Kyoto is famous for its celebrities and has been least affected by the warfare and bombings. They bought a lot of things there and invited me downstairs to take a look. The most valuable one is *Saturn Peach Temple Fair*, a large painting of over ten square meters by Qiu Ying, a renowned Chinese artist of the Ming Dynasty. The painting is delicately mounted and produces an unrivaled sight. Another painting of ancient beauties by the same artist, and two paintings of horses by Zhao Mengfu of the late-Song/early-Yuan Dynasties, are also quite attractive. They also bought a beautifully decorated sword about one meter long as a gift to me, and presented it in a small but serious ceremony. I said, "An ancient saying goes, 'face-powder for a beauty, while a treasured sword for a hero', but I am not a hero, unfortunately." Dr. Gu said, "You represent the 450 million Chinese people and millions of our compatriots who were killed in the War, to come and punish the prime culprits in the capital of their country. What in the world can be more heroic than this?" I said, in the Peking opera, the official with a sword bestowed by the emperor could execute the criminals first and then report to the emperor. But we are now living in an era of the rule of law, where all arch-criminals must be tried before execution; otherwise, I wish I could kill a few to appease my hatred of the evil war criminals!

We chatted for a while and had lunch together in the canteen. We agreed to gather at Gen. Wang's office (China's Liaison Office) at 3:30 p.m. to set off for a cocktail party to be held at 5 o'clock by Robert L. Eichelberger, Commander of the US Eighth Army, at his private residence in Yokohama.

I went back for a nap. It was already 3:15 p.m. when I woke up, so I hurried to Gen. Wang's office.

There were five Chinese officials invited to the party. With Adjutant Luo included, the six of us took the two cars of Gen. Wang's and mine. After over an hour's drive, we arrived at Eichelberger's villa in Yokohama just before 5 o'clock.

Gen. Eichelberger and his Eighth Army fought in the European and Pacific arenas, winning numerous battles and performing meritorious service, which has gained him high reputation and status in the US army. He is now in charge of the garrison in the area of Yokohama and Tokyo. This party, with a lot of senior officials and celebrities from the Allied Powers invited, was but a gesture of friendship and hospitality on the part of Eichelberger. However, as there were not many big international gatherings in Tokyo, this party naturally became a major event and made a hit in town.

While we did not arrive late, the villa had already been full of distinguished guests. Fortunately, there was a huge lawn facing the beach, where those who did not join the crowd inside could look around and chat with each other.

Since Gen. Wang has been stationed in the GHQ for five years starting with a post in the Philippines, and also because he is a graduate of West Point, he met up with a lot of old and new friends, even his former classmates, and was fully occupied at the party. As for me, when I entered the house, my colleges, Lord Patrick from the UK and the acting president Northcroft from New Zealand, found me and led me to Gen. Eichelberger.

Dr. Gu came with me to greet Gen. Eichelberger, and was wrongly introduced as "Dr. Mei's secretary." But he did not mind and was even pleased, saying that this was the only way to get things done. "You are now a prominent figure in Tokyo, respected and having a car at your service," said he, "I can take advantage of the convenience given by your position to cover and perform my job (which is to investigate the factories, resources, scientific facilities, and culture and education in Japan). If you are asked who I am, you should just tell them I am your secretary." Dr. Gu is a humorous and obliging person. Since I came to Tokyo, he has accompanied and taken care of me, and this was not the first time that he had been mistaken for my secretary. I agreed to his tactic. Should he put on airs because of his identity as the former Vice Minister of Education or the president of the National Central University, he might be kept at a respectful distance and find it difficult to get anything achieved. I think this practical approach is what anyone who works abroad should understand and learn from.

Gen. Eichelberger is about 60 years old, quite tall, who looks sincere and amiable. He expressed happiness and appreciation for our coming to his party. He told us that he had visited China twice, the first time in 1920, the ninth year of the Republic of China, when he performed his duty in North and Northeast China and established solid relations with Tang Shaoyi and Li Jia'ao (the then supervisor of the Chinese Eastern Railway). His second visit to China was last year after the victory of the War, when he made a global tour with a stop in Shanghai. Also, he expressed his sincere enthusiasm and hope for China. It is both China's and the US' established national policy that the two countries should develop a friendly relationship and assist each other, which must be known to all American senior officials like Gen. Eichelberger; therefore, this kind of remarks will definitely be made whenever a conversation with them takes place.

The crowd of guests became larger. Among those who approached me, many were officers of the International Prosecution Section (IPS) and the prosecutors from different Allied Powers, who all seemed to know me, perhaps because of my recognizable mustache that I have kept since arriving in Tokyo. The prosecution staff would, of course, like to make contact with the judges, which is also necessary for their work, although in the common law theory, there is a taboo on any close relationship between judges and prosecutors.

We also met two renowned American educators and scholars: George D. Stoddard, President of the New York University, and Mr. Andrews, an economist. Mr. Stoddard is leading a 25-member delegation of educators, who have been invited by Gen. MacArthur to inspect the Japanese educational system and assist the GHQ in formulating Japan's postwar education policy. He has been in Japan for two weeks, and is now busy drafting a report before his planned departure in two days. He said that to reform Japan's education and ideology was difficult and complicated, but was also a most important issue at present. Mr. Andrews is a member of the delegation. He said that education was the only possible starting point to eradicate Japan's invasive mindset, its sense of superiority and the danger of its going on the wrong track. Messrs. Stoddard and Andrews are men of letters with gracious manners, and our conversation was very pleasant. Dr. Gu, on behalf of the Chinese government, invited them to take this opportunity to visit China, which they highly appreciated but declined due to the inconvenience in terms of timing and transportation. They said that they hoped to organize a special delegation to China. I responded that such a delegation should stay in China for a longer time, as a trip for 3 to 5 days would not yield substantial results. To end a more or less awkward topic in this way seemed to make everyone satisfied.

In addition, we met some senior military officers from the Soviet Union, who were the Soviet representatives to the Allied Council for Japan. We were introduced to each other, shook hands and exchanged some courtesy words. However, the bitter quarrels within the UN Security Council are widely reported in the newspapers these days, the Soviet troops are still lingering in China's northeast region where the Kuomintang (KMT) and the Communist Party of China (CPC) have frictions, all these put a barrier between us and prevented us from having an in-depth talk. But I believe that China and the Soviet Union have to get along well with each other, and this barrier will surely be removed someday.

We bade farewell to our host at around 6 o'clock and left the cocktail party. On our way back, we stopped by at the house of Gen. Wang's former employee, so as to take a look at a Japanese home.

It took us over an hour to arrive at the hotel, almost 8 o'clock when we started our dinner at the canteen.

Afterwards, I came across Justice Northcroft and Lord Patrick, who were eager to tell me that Gen. Eichelberger had invited us six judges to take his plane for a bird's eye view of the middle and southern parts of Japan, including Mount Fuji, Hiroshima (the aftermath of the atomic bombing) and Mount Sakurajima (the biggest active volcano in Japan). The plane, to be driven by Col. Donnold, Gen. Eichelberger's private pilot, will take off at 9 o'clock tomorrow morning, and we should therefore gather at 7 o'clock in the hotel and head for the airport. However, we need not worry about transportation as Gen. Eichelberger will send his adjutant to pick us up. They also told me, it was such a special treatment and a good opportunity of an air travel around Japan that I should never miss it. Alas, this is what I have been looking forward to, and I of course happily accepted the invitation. We then requested the canteen host to advance tomorrow's breakfast to 6:30 and serve it in our rooms.

I returned to my room, wrote in my diary and went to bed immediately, for I will have to get up very early tomorrow.

March 30, 1946, Saturday

My door was knocked by a waitress. From the window I could see the sun shining its light again. What a fine day today! After washing and eating in a rush, I went downstairs together with Justice Northcroft, my next door neighbor. Lord Patrick and Justice B.V.A. Röling from the Netherlands were already there waiting. The four of us took the car and it was 8:30 a.m. when we arrived at the airport.

Gen. Eichelberger had sent several staff members to take care of this flight at the airport and had arranged two army photographers and a reporter to go with us. We chatted with them for a while and also spoke with Col. Donnold, who invited us to board the plane at 9 o'clock sharp. The Americans have an acute sense of time: they do things according to an exact timetable, and such punctuality can be seen everywhere. As from a Chinese perspective, though, a pleasure flight like this one, with only a few passengers, should not have to follow an exact timetable, otherwise it could be deemed as too rigid. Indeed, to be punctual is a merit of the Americans. Every matter, big or small, should be seriously treated.

We took a B-17 Flying Fortress named Miss Em II, Gen. Eichelberger's special plane for his personal use only. Last year, he went on a vacation tour around the world by this plane, which was also piloted by Col. Donnold. Donnold told us that Gen. Eichelberger seldom used his plane to treat guests, so this invitation was indeed a special one. We responded to him with a smile.

Despite its intimidating name Flying Fortress and four power engines, the plane does not have a large capacity, with only five formal sofa seats. Even so, it is fully equipped: a radio set, an electric stove, couches, deck-chairs, and anything you name it. Also, there is a small bookshelf holding Eichelberger's favorite books, including several novels. "What a comfortable life it is for the US military men!" I thought.

A Fortress, as its name implies, is a fortress. From taking off to landing, it was smooth and steady, much easier than my flight from Chungking to Shanghai by China National Aviation Corporation and that from Shanghai to Tokyo by the A.T.C.

Upon departure from Atsugi Airport, we first flew around Yokohama. Yokohama used to be an important industrial city in Japan, but about 80% of its factories were bombed and burned into ruins. None of the surviving factory chimneys seemed belching smoke now.

Off Yokohama and the Fuji Bay, we saw the famous Mount Fuji, which looked like an old man wearing a traditional Chinese hood with white snow on top. Mount Fuji is the highest mountain in Japan and has been regarded as its symbol. After flying in a circle around it, we headed for Nagoya, which looked quite the same as Yokohama in terms of the devastation inflicted on it. However, a region adjacent to the destroyed industrial zone seemed not much affected by the bombings. I asked the officer assigned to accompany us what the reason was, and he said it was a residential area. From this we can see the humanitarian consideration and targeting accuracy of the US military in its aerial bombing operations. I hope he was not babbling. In fact, I was told later that it was a zone for shipbuilding, which was intentionally preserved by the American forces.

From Nagoya, we flew to Osaka and circled around it. Osaka was no smaller than Chicago in size and should also be an important industrial city, but only less than one-third of it was destroyed, for reasons unknown to me.

Over Kyoto, we could see that the city was almost immune from aerial bombings, with no observable traces of destruction at all. It was said that Kyoto was a city of culture and the Allied Powers decided not to bombard it. No wonder Dr. Gu, Gen. Wang and my fellow judges who visited Kyoto a few days ago all spoke so high of it!

From Kyoto we flew over Kobe, which seemed even more severely damaged than Yokohama and Nagoya.

Past Akashi, Awajishima and many other small islands, we headed for Hiroshima to see what the atomic bomb did to that city. It was quite a long flight. The plane went sometimes over the land and sometimes above the sea, so it was a little turbulent, at least not as smooth as before. It was very interesting to overlook those small islands rising and falling like waves, and the vast land with paddy-fields neatly arranged, each in the shape of a square or rectangle with almost the same size, crisscrossing as if drawn by a carpenter's ink marker. They are completely different from the messily demarcated farmlands in China.

I have not conducted any research on Japan, but I have some observations after seeing the layout of paddies. First, the Japanese peasants must be very hard-working, for they have cultivated all parcels of land, including those on the cliffs, and turned them into farmlands. Secondly, the Japanese government must have imposed strict regulations on the farmers and re-arranged their lands, otherwise the fields would not be in such a neat and uniform pattern with the same sizes and straight boundary lines. Thirdly, although Japan claimed that its land were barren and over-populated, using that as an excuse for invasion, their farmers must be leading a more comfortable life as compared with our Chinese rural population, judging from the image of the thousands of villages as we looked down from the plane. They lived in small bungalows, with wooden floors, glass windows, fences and gardens. They did not dress badly, and they looked strong and healthy (of course we could not see what they ate). Such living standards are already much higher than those of ordinary Chinese peasants, not to mention that this is the scenario after many years of war. Had Japan not engaged in wars and the warlords not squeezed them tightly, these peasants would not have found it hard to make a living. As to China, in contrast, the problems of poverty in the countryside are really serious!

From the plane, we could see Hiroshima covered in debris and rubble. Within an area of dozens of square kilometers, the once high-rise buildings had all fallen down to the ground without any living things around. Occasionally, there were a few buildings standing out, but only as skeletons with empty insides. The land was scorched, and not a single tree or grass could be seen. People had never expected that an atomic bomb in egg size would have such a terrible power. Should there be a third world war, I suspect that the human race would simply perish.

We talked a lot about the power of atomic bombs in the plane. It was rumored that the atomic bombing would turn a blind into a sighted person or vice versa, that a rooster could lay eggs and a barren woman could become pregnant. Incredible as they were, the stories were told and heard without being taken seriously.

After Hiroshima, the plane flew past Fukuoka and came to Takushima, and the big volcano on the island of Sakurajima was just around the corner. The Chinese word for "volcano" means "fire mountain"; however, there was no fire, only white smoke emitting from the crater. The smoke was heavy and fast, spiraling up very high (over 10,000 feet, I thought) and making a spectacular scene. Our plane flew around the smoke by drawing five circles from the top to the bottom of it. As we reached the lowest part, we saw the volcano breathing out fire and stones as if in a rage. The closer we got, the more smoke it seemed to be emitting. We watched it intensively and silently, and did not look away until it was finally out of sight. All the four of us believed that it was a wonder of the universe, which highlighted our tour today.

It was almost 1:00 p.m. We became a little tired and hungry, so the attendant gave us some food for lunch. After that, we all felt sleepy and took a rest, except for looking occasionally out of the windows. I really fell asleep and snored as they told me later.

After seeing the volcano, the plane adjusted its direction and headed back to Tokyo. When we were near Yokohama, as it was not yet 5:00 p.m., we asked Col. Donnold to fly over the Imperial Palace in Tokyo for a bird's eye view. He agreed and made the plane circle around it. I do not know what my three companions thought, but for me, who had lived in Peking for many years, such a palace was not so impressive. It was neither magnificent nor gorgeous, looking more like a mountain fortress or blockhouse whose main function seemed only to defend against violent rebellions or assassinations.

It was already 6 o'clock when the plane landed at Atsugi Airport. We extended our sincere thanks to Col. Donnold and the other officers who took care of us during the tour, and drove back to the hotel for dinner at 7:30.

Japan is a small country in size. In today's 9-hour non-stop flight, we already saw most of it and, moreover, the most representative parts of it, especially Mount Fuji, Hiroshima, Sakurajima volcano, and the Imperial Palace in Tokyo. The four of us were extraordinarily satisfied, and bade "end of a happy day" to each other after dinner.

In less than ten minutes after stepping into my room, I received a telephone call from Xiang Mingsi, who is staying upstairs in this hotel. As it turned out, he had come back to Tokyo from Shanghai tonight with the convenience of Mr. Keenan's private aircraft. He also brought with him Mr. Fang Fushu, a lawyer and English secretary in the Ministry of Foreign Affairs, whom I had requested to come to my assistance. I immediately invited them to my room, and we chatted pleasantly about some state affairs and our recent journeys. In about half an hour, a room was arranged for Fang at the Daiichi Hotel. He therefore left along with Mr. Liu Zijian, a secretary additionally recruited by Mingsi.

Dr. Gu was still in high spirits, so he invited Danru, Mingsi and me to have a drink in a Japanese pub. We talked further about the situation in China until 10 o'clock. Coming back to the hotel, I was so tired that I fell fast asleep shortly after.

March 31, 1946, Sunday

It was another sunny day. Looking out of the windows, I was excited because Danru, Yiqiao and I planned to go to Atami hot springs this afternoon and stay there for one night.

After breakfast, Danru walked to my room in haste, saying that he received a telegram from Shanghai: Gen. Zhu Shiming, China's representative to the Allied Council for Japan, and his entourage of about twenty people were taking a Chinese plane for Tokyo which would arrive at Atsugi Airport at about 3 or 4 o'clock this afternoon. Danru is China's liaison officer in Tokyo, who of course had to stay here to welcome and take care of Gen. Zhu's delegation. As such, we had to cancel our planned trip to Atami.

In the morning, Yiqiao came for a short while; so did Mingsi. Yiqiao said that since a Chinese special plane was coming to Tokyo, he would like to take advantage and go back to Shanghai with it. We tried to persuade him to stay as his work in Tokyo went well with a lot of valuable materials collected. Meanwhile, he was also hesitant about leaving.

Mingsi and I invited the two newcomer secretaries, Fang and Liu, for lunch at our hotel. Then I took a nap, read the newspapers and wrote in my diary. At 4:00 p.m., Yiqiao and I went to the airport to welcome Gen. Zhu's delegation. When we arrived, there had already been many people waiting there, among whom Gen. Wang was the busiest.

After about an hour, a plane painted with the Chinese national emblem appeared and hovered above the airport. This was the first time that a plane flown by us Chinese landed on Japan's soil (China had once sent a fleet of aircraft during the war to disseminate leaflets, without landing), which was really memorable.

When the plane came to a stop, we shook hands with Gen. Zhu, and greeted and praised Col. Yi, the aircraft captain. After dinner back at the hotel, I watched a movie together with Yiqiao and Mingsi in the small theater on the first floor. Then I took a shower and went to bed at 10:30. When Gen. Zhu came to the hotel for a return visit, I was already fast asleep and did not even hear the telephone ringing.

April 1, 1946, Monday

Today's weather was also good. Quickly skimming through two English newspapers, I found no mention of Gen. Zhu's arrival by a Chinese special plane. What a shame! Our country's intelligence and publicity work was too poor. I did not see even a Chinese reporter at the airport yesterday; no wonder there was nothing about it in these English newspapers.

After breakfast, Dr. Gu came to tell me that he would take the Chinese plane back to Shanghai tomorrow morning, which made me anxious, because I had planned to ask him to take some letters for mailing in China. It is also a shame when mentioning the correspondence between China and Japan. There are many Chinese in Japan, and it has been over six months since Japan's surrender, but there is still no normal channel established for correspondence between the two countries. Some people have been here for two or three months, but have not received any family letters. There seems to be no reliable way other than requesting friends to carry them back and forth.

Since Yiqiao was set to go tomorrow, I had to quickly write my letters. Hardly had I finished two, to my father and my wife Wanru respectively, when there came Messrs. Li Jizhi [Li Ji] and Zhang Fengju [Zhang Dinghuang], both being delegates from the Ministry of Education who accompanied Gen. Zhu to Tokyo yesterday. We had lunch together in the canteen. In the afternoon, Yiqiao and I went to Ginza, seeking to buy some presents for families and friends. April 15 will be my first wedding anniversary, which is just around the corner. Living far apart from each other, I have to buy Wanru something lovely as a gift. However, today's Japan is no longer what it was like in the past, and good stuff is rarely seen. After searching in one shop after another, I finally found a red flower carved out of ivory in the Mitsukoshi Store (the largest department store in Tokyo). It was not perfect, and neither was it cheap. Fortunately, when I produced my name card to show my identity, they did not require me to pay taxes, which would be costlier than the ivory flower itself. Yiqiao laughed and said that the title "Honorable Justice" was quite respected and awe-inspiring in Tokyo. We also bought some Japanese postal stamps, paper fans and toys for our relatives, friends, and their children in China.

In the evening, Gen. Zhu invited us to his residence for dinner. The place was delicately constructed, which used to be the private mansion of the Japanese Minister of Agriculture and Forestry. Having arrived here only yesterday, Gen. Zhu hadn't got time to put the place in good order yet. Also present at the dinner were all the people who came with Gen. Zhu yesterday. Afterwards we chatted for a while, and it was already 9:30 p.m. when I returned to the hotel.

In a haste I wrapped up the ivory flower for Wanru and the other presents, and wrote letters to friends, including Sun Ke [or as Sun Fo] (president of the Legislative Council), Zhang Boping [Zhang Qinglan], Ren Yingshi, Wu Yifei, Wu Desheng, and Dai Yifu.

It was midnight when I took the package to Yiqiao's room. He insisted that I should stay for a talk, which was soon joined by Mingsi. We chatted until 1:30 a.m., about the chaos that China was facing and our concern, as well as our idea that China should stand on guard against Japan despite of its defeat. In this emotional atmosphere, we bade farewell and encouraged each other to put utmost efforts into our respective work.

April 2, 1946, Tuesday

At 10 o'clock this morning, the Tokyo Tribunal held a judges' conference. I thought this would be a good opportunity for Secretary Fang to see the Tribunal's office and be introduced to the judges and the staff. He came to my hotel at 9:30 a.m., and we rode in my car to the former War Ministry Building. Having arrived at 10:00 and after leading him to the office for my personal secretary next to my own room, I went to the conference room immediately.

The matters reported and discussed at the meeting today were not very important.

It was reported that, in the opinion of Gen. Douglas MacArthur, sending people to visit the Nuremberg Trial was not practical due to time constraints. Regarding the appointment of three language arbiters (to determine the accuracy of translations between English and Japanese) and the recruitment of American counsel (about twenty in number) for the defendants, they were in the process of being actively selected. As for the Tribunal's request for a general secretary, MacArthur had agreed and suggested that the position be filled by a local judge from Detroit. However, my fellow judges considered that person underqualified, and advised him to find another one, while the Tribunal itself would also try to identify a candidate.

The matter discussed at the meeting was the weather in summer. This is a serious topic because, based on its current rate of progress, the open trial cannot be started until May, and we will have to spend the summer here. All the judges are afraid of the summer heat, especially McDougall. Indeed, here in Tokyo, the temperature can reach as high as 90 °F, and the judges will have to sit on the bench for several long hours every day, wearing robes and facing the piercing camera light, without the comfort of air conditioning. What an unbearable situation!

During the discussion, a medical specialist from the GHQ was invited to give some explanations and answer our inquiries. But the meeting achieved nothing material, except that all of us thought MacArthur's proposal for the court to adjourn for two months from July to August was unreasonable. Finally, we decided to request the GHQ to install an air conditioning system quickly, and to ban the continuous lighting of the spotlights for film-shooting. We also believed that the trial sessions should be started earlier in the morning, and that longer weekend trips for relaxation would also be necessary.

After the meeting, I introduced my secretary Fang to the judges and some key staff. He was welcomed by everyone, especially Higgins who showed the highest sincerity.

Back at the hotel canteen for lunch, I ran into Mr. Yu Junji, who was en route for the US and then Italy, where he will serve as the Chinese ambassador. He had just flown from Chungking, and it was a great pleasure to see him again in this foreign land. As he was in a hurry to catch a flight to the US at Atsugi Airport, we bade farewell to each other right after lunch.

Having taken a nap, I read the newspapers and a book for about three hours, and chatted with Mr. Keenan via the telephone. At 6 o'clock, I went down to the bar to talk with the other judges. I told them that I would like to hold a small cocktail party in my room at 6:00 p.m. tomorrow. I also said that Gen. Wang would be invited to display the paintings and other artistic objects he had collected, especially *Saturn Peach Temple Fair*, the famous painting by Qiu Ying. They were very pleased with my offer. We had dinner together and talked at the hotel corridor, when someone came to tell us that Justice Henri Bernard, the French judge, had arrived. We asked our acting president Northcroft to pay him a visit on our behalf and invite him downstairs to meet us. After a while, Northcroft came back with a sulky face, telling us that Bernard had already put on his bathrobe and wanted to go to sleep after a bath, so they only exchanged a few words. In addition, he said that Bernanrd's English was barely understandable to him, which would be a problem for our meetings in future. Well, we still have no idea how well the Russian judge speaks English, but I am sure there will be many different accents with which English is spoken among us, making a quite interesting scene.

At nearly 9 o'clock, Patrick felt he had caught a cold, so we parted company there. McDougall and I went to the small theater in the hotel, but I left in less than ten minutes as the movie was boring. Back in my room, I caught up on writing in my diary, played Tai-Chi and went to bed after taking a shower.

Since the second day of my arrival in Japan, I have never stopped playing Tai-Chi, which I am pretty proud of. However, I did not play it at a fixed time of the day, but mostly in the morning and sometimes at night. Maybe it is not so healthy to do it before going to bed. Yet, I must continue with it, especially because my status as a judge prevents me from wandering around, while I have to ride in a car wherever I go. In this case, I have to keep this minimal exercise, not to mention that I have a history of practicing it for two years.

April 3, 1946, Wednesday

I invited Secretary Fang to my hotel this morning. Together we studied *Charter of the International Military Tribunal for the Far East*. After discussion and explanation, I handed the text to him for translation into Chinese. He had been a little bored lately for having nothing to do, and I thought this translation job would keep him busy for a few days. Fang is hard-working and has a good knowledge of English and law. I believe that he can give me a great deal of assistance when the Tribunal officially starts its trial sessions.

Before lunch, I went to the bar and found all my fellow judges there, including the newcomer from France, Justice Bernard. He is about 50 years old, of medium build, wearing glasses, with no beard or mustache. There are three or four gold teeth in his mouth. His English is not good, but I managed to understand him when I paid close attention to what he said. He looked sincere in his attitude, quite different from a typical Frenchman or Parisian that I had seen or that people had imagined. I told him that I visited France and stayed in Paris for a while seventeen years ago. He was very pleased to hear it, so we started to talk about Paris. We were all engaged in joyful conversations and, before we realized it, it was past 1:30 p.m., the end of the canteen's lunch hours. Nevertheless, the seven of us walked in single file to the canteen for lunch. Since we have almost formed a special group, a "privileged class" in this Imperial Hotel, the canteen's manager and waitresses often give us exceptional treatments. Despite that the lunch time had passed, the plates and forks were still readily placed on the so-called "Judges' Table" and the waitresses were still waiting there with smiles on their faces.

Japanese waitresses are really gentle and humble, always smiling and bowing to guests, especially to those from the Allied Powers. I wonder whether it is the nature of Japanese women to do so, or is more or less used as a "honey trap."

It was already 2:30 when we finished lunch. I was about to take a nap, when a phone call came from the manager's room, saying that a military officer sent by the GHQ wanted to deliver me a letter which required my acknowledgement with signature. He asked whether the officer could be allowed to come to my room, and I of course said yes. The officer soon came, gave me that letter in a polite manner, and produced two pieces of paper for my signature.

The letter was written by Major General Stephen J. Chamberlin, Chief of Staff of the GHQ. With nice wording, it says that Gen. MacArthur has just returned to his office from a severe illness, and that he is pleased that I am in Japan and wishes me well in Tokyo. It continues that MacArthur wishes to invite me for luncheon, the exact date to be communicated later.

While being a kind of courtesy letter, it showed how judges are respected in a nation under the rule of law.

After reading for two hours, it was 5:30 when Gen. Wang arrived.

He helped me arrange the room and the seats, and prepare drinks and snacks. We also ordered three kinds of alcohol—Australian whisky, Japanese saki, and beer. It was a pity that we did not have Maotai, Daqu, and Shaoxing wine for this party; otherwise it would be extraordinarily exotic. Gen. Wang had brought over his paintings.

At 6 o'clock, all my colleagues came except Justice Higgins who had a pre-arranged appointment. Gen. Wang is a party expert; he helped me to take good care of these guests. When he explained the Chinese calligraphy and paintings, the audience was amazed and fascinated. The ancient painting *Saturn Peace Temple Fair* is one of China's greatest artworks, which opened the eyes of my fellow judges and made a strong impression on them.

We talked and drank until 7:30, when we went downstairs for dinner. After that, Mingsi and I went to Danru's room and chatted until 11 o'clock. We worried and couldn't help sighing over the situation in China, especially the military conflicts in the northeast region and the economic crisis. The heavy sacrifices in the past eight years have earned China a reasonable status in the international arena. If we cannot work hard together in the construction of our country, this status will decline and eventually be lost. Such a thought made me trembling with fear. For people like us who stay in a foreign land, this kind of feeling is most acute, and this kind of apprehension most vivid. With these things dwelling in my mind, I could not fall asleep for two or three hours tonight.

April 4, 1946, Thursday

At 10:00 a.m., along with Wang Danru and Xiang Mingsi, I went to visit Gen. Zhu Gongliang [Zhu Shiming]. We only talked about the issue of lodging. Since judges and prosecutors cannot stay in the same place, Mingsi must leave the Imperial Hotel. He decided to move into the house where Danru was set to live, and it was said that Mrs. Wang would also come from Australia within this month. As for me, I have decided to remain in the Imperial Hotel, because the judges from eight other Allied Powers are all staying and have formed a special group there. Gen. Zhu fully agreed to my idea, and told me that he would welcome me to stay with him if there should be any inconveniences with the hotel. He also said that he could arrange a separate accommodation for me if I would bring my family over. I thanked him for his great kindness.

Gen. Zhu is China's chief representative to the Allied Council for Japan, which means that he is the top Chinese official stationed in Japan. In accordance with the Chinese presidential order, all the Chinese officials here, whether military or civilian, are under his supervision and control, with the only exception of the judge of the International Military Tribunal for the Far East. He is also the only counterpart to deal with Gen. MacArthur's GHQ, and is in charge of all the work concerning China's military, political, economic and cultural affairs in Japan. Needless to say, he has an arduous job and a great task. The team that he brought the day before has less than twenty members, but it is said that there will be two more groups joining him within this month. My Japanese secretary Mr. Luo Jiyi will also arrive in a couple of days. However, as the trial work is yet to start, there may not be appropriate assignments for him for the time being. I asked Gen. Zhu to give Luo a temporary job at the Allied Council, to which he agreed happily.

The Allied Council for Japan will hold its first meeting tomorrow, and Gen. Zhu has preparatory work to do, so we said good-bye after only half an hour's visit with him.

Mingsi told me that the IPS would have a chartered plane to Shanghai tomorrow or the day after. I went back to the hotel quickly and wrote several letters to my families and friends, to be taken to China by the IPS plane. One of the letters was to Mr. Sun Ke, to which I attached the article by Owen Lattimore. Sun loves reading and always pays close attention to international affairs. During his years in Chungking, whenever he read a good article, he would ask his secretary to type out and distribute it to his subordinates and friends. When I lived in Chungking, I received his distributions at least once or twice every month. I believe this eloquent piece of Lattimore's will also be distributed by him, or even have it translated for publication. As such, he will not be the only one to whom I have introduced this article. From the bottom of my heart, I hope that all people of insight will really understand Japan and become aware as early as possible of its potential threat to China.

In the afternoon, the hotel manager Morris came and suggested that I could move to a more spacious, quieter and cooler room, since summer was approaching and he knew that I would stay here for a long time. Some twenty rooms became available as a US cultural and educational investigation delegation had just went home.

I was not unsatisfied with this room, but Morris' suggestion moved me. He then showed me a few, and I selected Suite No. 256 facing south and east next to the garden. Like the current one, it also has three parts: a large living room, a bedroom and a bathroom. All the utensils are provided in double sets, and the telephone has two receivers in the living room and the bedroom respectively. In addition, in the living room, there are two dressing mirrors as well as a running-water sink behind a folding screen, which are meant for the guests to have a quick tidy-up.

I suspect that such a suite would cost at least *fabi* 20,000 per day in a big hotel in Shanghai, which means that the monthly salary of a mid-level official or a college professor would only cover one week's rental, with nothing left. I cannot help sighing. Is China's politics to go bankrupt? Does the Chinese government want to leave our civil servants, teachers and other intellectuals to die of poverty and hunger? A defeated country like Japan has found means to tackle its difficulties, or at least it is trying to look for such means. On the other hand, China, on the winning side and supposedly one of the "Four Big Powers," ridiculously does not know what to do and cannot find a way out. What a shame!

At 4 o'clock in the afternoon, I went to China's Liaison Office to read the news dispatches for these days. (These are collected and published by the Chinese Central News Agency in Tokyo, the only source of information about China apart from the two English newspapers provided by the GHQ.) There were reports on the Communist army attacking and taking over certain places, some officials being transferred to head a certain province or bureau, etc.—none of the things that would arouse my excitement. So I had come with high hopes for this visit but left in great disappointment. I should have expected that!

At dusk, I joined the other judges in the bar. After dinner, I went with Danru to Earnie Pyle Theater next door to the hotel to watch shows and movies. The "generals' box" was at the left corner of the balcony, but there was no one else there, as if it were set for the exclusive use of the two of us. It is said that there are less than ten American generals in Japan, and that the US military ranks are strictly controlled. A brigadier general or major general is already considered high-ranking, while there are only a few dozens of lieutenant generals and full generals in the whole United States. As for the Generals of the Army, there are only three, with Douglas MacArthur being one of them. The other two are Dwight Eisenhower, who led the army to fight in Europe and defeat Nazi Germany, and George Marshall, who is now representing the US government in China in its efforts to mediate the conflict between the KMT and the CPC.

Although there were only the two of us in the "generals' box," the theater was crowded with an audience (all being US military officers—the Japanese are not allowed here), the steam was too hot and the air too stuffy, so we retreated before the movie finished.

Back in my room, I wrote in my diary, played Tai-Chi and went to bed after bathing.

April 5, 1946, Friday

Secretary Fang came in the morning, and we discussed the translation of some terms in the Charter. After that, we decided to go out as the weather was really good. We went to Kanda (my favorite culture street) by car, wandered in the book stores and walked through the street to feel the warmth of sunshine. My old car has been replaced with a black one, having a steel plate of China's national emblem hanging in front. Wallace was very happy to drive this new car.

In the street we found a Chinese restaurant, a quite large one, and we walked in to take a rest. The owner, at about 30, was from Ningbo. He told us in detail what Japan was like during the War and the miserable pictures of the Tokyo bombings. He said that the Japanese used to bully the Chinese in Japan by every means, but after China's victory, the situation improved a lot. He said that, shortly after Japan's surrender, he seized a Japanese who had attacked him before to his restaurant and beat him black and blue as a revenge. Indeed, our protection of the Chinese living in Japan has not yet unfolded, and their life is still not easy. I will definitely relate this matter to Gen. Zhu Gongliang.

Having strolled around the culture street, we drove to Ginza, and window-shopped at some department stores like Matsuya and Mitsukoshi, where goods were few and prices high. The stores were not very big in the first place, much inferior to the department stores in Shanghai such as Sincere, Wing On, Sun Sun and The Sun, and they became even more cramped after the War. There were a lot of people in the stores, and the streets were also crowded. The Japanese looked quite strong, especially the young women. They seemed to be indifferent to the US soldiers, as if not knowing who had conquered whom. Is this a success or failure of MacArthur's policy?—Only History will tell.

After lunch and a nap in the hotel, Mingsi and Danru came along with Li Jizhi, Zhang Fengju and Xie Nanguang, to discuss the gains and losses of the US policies on the control of Japan as well as the attitude that should be adopted by China. Li, Zhang and Xie accompanied Gen. Zhu to attend the first meeting of the Allied Council for Japan this morning, so they had an awful lot of thoughts in their mind. They told me that MacArthur was stern and proud at today's meeting, striving in his speech to justify his lenient policies and denounce all unreasonable criticism from the outside. He left right after he spoke, and the meeting was then chaired by a US deputy representative. The proposals prepared by the Soviet Union were struck down one after another, which constituted another example of the various disputes and conflicts between the US and the Soviet Union all over the world.

After they left, I went to the bar to talk with my fellow judges, and got ready to attend Mr. Keenan's banquet together.

We went there at 7:30 p.m. The banquet was held inside the hotel, which was very convenient for us. Apart from the judges and prosecutors from the Allied Powers, only a few reporters and photographers were invited.

Keenan is very much of a politician. As soon as he saw me, he began to speak eloquently about his pleasant trip in China and the honor he had to meet President Chiang Kai-shek and First Lady Soong May-ling. He said that Gen. MacArthur had asked him to invite me for a dinner and talk, and that he was considering a suitable date.

In the banquet, he raised his glass to toast the leaders of each of the Allied Powers, and introduced the judges and prosecutors present there. He gave everyone generous compliments and praises, and expressed special respect for us from China. The photographers took quite a few pictures, for publicity's sake, of course. However, while talking cheerfully and humorously, Keenan did not even mention a word about the question that concerned the judges most: When will the Indictment be officially submitted? Some judges have become impatient with waiting. This is what the judges are most unhappy about.

Present at the banquet tonight was also a prosecutor from the Philippines, because under the revised Charter, the Philippines and India can each send a judge and a prosecutor to participate in the Trial. Initially, the nine judges were representatives of the signatories to Japan's Instrument of Surrender, while the current eleven judges include all member countries of the Far Eastern Commission in Washington, DC.

There is still no news of the Soviet judge, and now we have to wait for two additional ones, which makes us even more anxious, as we have had nothing to do in Tokyo. It does not bother me too much as it was only two weeks ago that I arrived, but some of my colleagues have been here for more than two months!

After the banquet, I returned to my room. Danru came to discuss matters such as the various tasks that China tries to do in Japan, the personnel issues and the organizational adjustments. I promised to make proposals to Gen. Zhu Gongliang tomorrow. We then discussed our plan for spending this weekend in Atami. When he left, I wrote in my diary and went to bed after midnight.

April 6, 1946, Saturday

The weather broke, drizzling continuously from early morning.

Opening the newspapers, I found reports on the meeting of the Allied Council for Japan, attended by the representatives of China, the US, the UK and the Soviet Union. As recounted by Li, Zhang and Xie yesterday, it showed the conflicts and contradictions between the US and the USSR. Mr. Ball, the British representative, kept flattering the United States. China was put in an awkward position; no wonder that Gen. Zhu would rather take a compromising attitude or just keep silent from time to time.

At 9:30 a.m., I went to visit Gen. Zhu Gongliang. Thanks to Wallace's good memory, we took the right way and arrived directly at the former private mansion of the Minister of Agriculture and Forestry, which has now become Gen. Zhu's residence and also the office of the Chinese Delegation.

Gongliang was here for nearly a week now, but there had not been a real chance for the two of us to have a good talk. As a matter of fact, in the recent five or six years back at home, we had only met with each other briefly for once or twice. This time he came to Japan for an extremely important mission, and the tasks he took charge of were arduous and challenging. "Layman" as I was on Japanese issues, with what I saw and heard plus some common sense, I was determined to follow the Chinese proverb "to tell all that I know and tell it without reserve."

So I made many comments on various issues concerning China's role in Japan, the personnel and organizational structure, and so forth. He was modest and expressed willingness to accept my suggestions.

Later we talked about the situation in China as well as some personal affairs. As it was past noontime, I invited him to have lunch with me at the Imperial Hotel. He changed out of his uniform into plain clothes and followed me. Given the nuisance of too many acquaintances in the dining hall, I ordered two meals to be served in my room. (His position and rank do not allow him to show his face everywhere; I have experienced it myself but to a lesser extent as I am but a civilian officer.) We talked after lunch until 3:00 p.m. when Danru came in. Gongliang took my car back while Danru and I set off in his car on our first journey to Atami for the weekend.

Atami is 80 or 90 miles away from Tokyo, and 50 or 60 miles from Yokohama. By the time when we started off, the road was already wet with a steady, drizzling rain. When we passed Yokohama, the rain became heavier and we could not drive at full speed. Even our emulative driver Howard (an American officer who usually drives for Danru) could do nothing about it. The cherries blossomed all along the road from Yokohama to Atami, lining up to welcome the guests with a cheerful fragrance. Danru said that it was right in the middle of the Japanese cherry blossom season, as in two weeks everything would be gone. I recall that Jiang Baili, a renowned Chinese general, once said that for the Japanese, "the man is samurai, the flower is cherry blossom." The fortune of this nation in the past few decades was just like the cherry flowers, one moment in full blossom, the next withering and falling away.

When passing Hakone, the evening lights were just lit up, and it was quite interesting to watch the rain through the windows of the car. Being a famous scenery spot, Hakone in the time of full cherry blossom was especially intoxicating. As the car progressed slowly, it went suddenly through a cave, and suddenly under a moon bridge. With birds singing and flowers radiating their fragrance everywhere, and with the rain pattering, I did suspect that I was traveling in a picture or in the fairyland. It is a pity that I don't have the talent of a poet or a painter to depict such a scene!

It was past 7 o'clock when we finally arrived at Atami. We put up for the night at an inn named "Daikokuya," run by a Chinese from Canton with the surname Ng. He was quite hospitable and solicitous for us, and he told us that he had resided in Japan for over two decades. After dinner, Danru went out to visit his friends. I felt a bit tired and went to bed at 10 o'clock after a hot spring bath.

Today is Saturday, and also the US Army Day when the American officers and soldiers have one day off. As a result, a very large number of American army men came to Atami for sightseeing, so that almost all the hotels were fully occupied by them. Even when I woke up at midnight, I could hear them singing American popular jazz songs.

Speaking of today's Army Day, I must add a description of a scene that I saw during the day. Early in the morning when I rode in the car to visit Gen. Zhu, I was stopped midway at the gate of Hibiya Park for about half an hour. The parading procession of American soldiers (presumably the US Eighth Army on garrison duty led by Gen. Eichelberger) extended as long as one mile, all in uniform and fully-armed, marching in perfect step. Behind thousands of infantrymen were the artillery and the machine gun corps, followed by the armored cars, the anti-aircraft artillery and the tank fleet in the rear. When proceeding, they pretended to take aim and howled in radio speakers from time to time. The atmosphere was highly tense, and the whole scene extremely magnificent, full of power and grandeur. When the parade passed across the downtown area of Tokyo, both American and Japanese policemen were there to maintain order as there was a thick hedge of spectators along the streets. Curious enough, I could see nothing on the faces of those Japanese men and women, old or young. As things should be, they would have felt resentful or shameful of this provoking massive demonstration of force, but on the contrary, there was no such sign at all. It is said that, since the landing of the American troops, there has not occurred even one "accident," which is probably because the Japanese nationals have, on average, a relatively high level of intelligence and knowledge, so they can understand the will of the Japanese government (and the Emperor) and obey its orders; or rather, it is a result of the Americans' lenient policy, which has convinced the Japanese to accept the occupation forces without much adverse sentiment. It is also reported that at the beginning of the occupation, Japanese people did feel ashamed and resentful; however, with the passing of time, they have become inured to the unusual and are no longer retaining strong emotions against it.

April 7, 1946, Sunday

Although Daikokuya is a Chinese hotel, its layout and decorations are totally Japanese. Last night, I slept on Tatami—Japanese mat flooring used as bed—for the first time in my life. I was so tired that I slept sound and comfortably till 8 o'clock in the morning, when the rain had stopped.

Breakfast was offered in Japanese cuisine, sumptuous but not entirely to my taste. I did not even dare to touch some of the dishes.

Atami being famous for its hot springs, I took another hot bath before returning to Tokyo with Danru by taking another road. This scenic highway wound up and down along the foot of Mount Fuji, with cherry fragrance permeating the air, and the snow-capped mountain above and the crystalline Fuji Lake below all coming into our view. Probably because it was Sunday and was in the cherry blossom season, this area attracted a large number of tourists, many of whom were young students.

A stretch of the road was very muddy, and our car got stuck in the mud helplessly. In front of us there was a big truck also being stuck, and its passengers—dozens of Japanese men and women on a spring outing—were standing aside and watching helplessly. It was much easier for our car to get out of the mud because of its small size. While we were struggling, some stronger Japanese men came up to give us a hand with great eagerness. They knew we were Chinese, but none of them looked gloomy or angry. Shortly after that came a giant lorry carrying thirty or forty American soldiers, who upon seeing this immediately jumped off to help push the truck. With concerted efforts, even the huge Japanese truck was moved out of the mud. People from all three vehicles were pleased at that time, with a meeting of hearts and full of goodwill toward one another. It was indeed a very touching scene, which impressed me deeply. "This is the way the Americans help the Japanese solve problems, regardless of whether the problems are big or small. No wonder they are so popular here in Japan," said Danru. In my view, the human world should be a blissful one if people and nations could genuinely help one another. Unfortunately, things do not go on as it should be. The world today, on the contrary, is still full of suspicion and hatred. I'm afraid that the seed of war and aggression could only be uprooted and destroyed after a long period of time.

When passing by Hakone again on our way back to Tokyo, we stepped off the car, went for a walk, and took a short break at Fuji Hotel. Hakone is indeed a picturesque resort, especially at this time of the year when cherry trees are in full blossom everywhere.

It was after noontime when we passed Yokohama, and 1:00 p.m. when we finally arrived at the Imperial Hotel. Hibiya Park opposite the hotel was surrounded by some twenty to thirty thousand people. I asked around and learned later that those were the leftists holding a mass rally against the Shidehara Cabinet. I also heard that clashes broke out between the protesters and the Japanese police, with fourteen policemen injured.

I took a nap after lunch. At about 4 o'clock, Zhu Gongliang, Li Jizhi and Zhang Fengju came for a visit. A few moments later, Xiang Mingsi and Wang Danru joined us. It was like what was described in an ancient Chinese prose poem, "All the persons of virtue have arrived." I ordered tea and snacks to entertain my guests. We kept talking up until 6:30 p.m., and Gen. Zhu invited us to a Chinese dinner at Tianbao Mansion, but the price there was high and the dishes not so delicious.

I came back to the hotel at 9 o'clock and ran into Higgins. We went for a movie in the small theater, which turned out to be a hustling musical drama. After the movie, we chatted for another hour at the bar, where McDougall and Röling joined us. It was as late as midnight when we retired for the night.

April 8, 1946, Monday

The weather turned sunny and bright again. I had not been to the Tribunal's office for almost a week now. In the morning, Secretary Fang came and handed me the draft Chinese translation of the Charter, and we rode in the car to the former War Ministry Building—our courthouse. I took a look at his translation, and chatted with McDougall, Patrick and Röling, who were all full of complaints about the judges' state of idleness as well as the prosecution's delay in submitting the Indictment. Besides, they were tired as the Soviet judge still had not arrived and, moreover, the Far Eastern Commission had increased the number of judges by two, i.e., representatives of Indian and the Philippines, which meant that the official trial would inevitably be further delayed.

I left the office at 11:00 a.m. and then visited the bookstores in Kanda together with Secretary Fang. I bought some old Japanese stamps, which I intended to enclose in my letters to friends and relatives in China for their kids to play with. I also strolled around Ginza, where pedestrians pushed and squeezed on the street, probably because the weather was so fine and spring was very much in the air. The walls of the department stores were posted with slogans and pictures of all the parties running election campaigns, most of which were artistic and delicate; those made by the communist party were especially eye-catching.

The day after tomorrow will be the national election day (to elect members of the National Diet), so the campaigns were exceedingly intensive these days. According to the forecast, it would be difficult for the left-wing radicals to rise, and victory might still go to those relatively progressive parties supporting Tennoism (the emperor system).

After lunch back in the hotel, Li Jizhi and Zhang Fengju came to discuss with me on how to raise the issue with the GHQ for the effective recovery of the Chinese antiquities and ancient books and records plundered to Japan during the War. They were sent here to take charge of this matter. I also contributed quite a few suggestions although it was not my immediate concern. They left a document of the United Nations on the recovery of such antiquities for me to study, as there were some legal issues in this matter.

Secretary Fang came in after they left. We planned to visit Ueno Tōshōgū in Ueno Park, but had to give up because Wallace couldn't find it. At around 5:00 p.m., I returned to the hotel, read some newspapers and wrote in my diary. I did not have dinner until 8 o'clock.

After dinner, I read a book on the trial of German war criminals for two hours, and went to Mingsi's room to talk with him for another hour. It was 12:30 a.m. when I went to bed after playing Tai-Chi and taking a shower.

Mingsi told me that the procurator from a certain country argued that the Emperor of Japan should be listed as a war criminal and indicted, which aroused a heated debate at the procurators' meeting today. The issue ended up getting tabled without being put to a vote for the time being. I said to Mingsi that this was a political issue; from a legal perspective, I could not see why the Emperor was not responsible for Japan's war of aggression. This issue had also been discussed several times among the judges in our private conversations, and many of them shared my view.

Mingsi was in agony because the pieces of evidence that China could provide were too few, while logically our evidence should take the largest share since Japan's invasion of China lasted for at least fifteen years.

April 9, 1946, Tuesday

When I opened the English newspapers first thing in the morning, a headline caught my eye: "Hungry Chinese Eating Bark, Rat Meat and Dirt," with subheadings "Three million people are starving to death in Hunan and other provinces" and "Gen. Chennault of the 'Flying Tigers' organized air-droppings of relief supplies." In addition, there were other conspicuous news from China, such as "KMT and CPC Competing to Occupy Changchun," "Large-Scale Civil War Being Started in Manchuria," "China Eagerly Expected Envoy Marshall's Return to China for Mediation of Civil War," and so forth.

The news was really disheartening. Indeed, those who are in foreign countries feel most painful to their own country's failure to live up to their expectations.

Knowing that the IPS would have a chartered plane to China in one or two days, I wrote six letters to my families and friends at home, in simple wording and just to give them my regards.

Secretary Fang came in the afternoon, saying that he would like to fly back to China by that chartered plane. I would agree in principle, but did not advise him to do so, considering that the court work might take a sudden turn and start quickly. Besides, the transportation between Japan and China was irregular and his returning date might be unpredictable. Therefore, this request could only be suspended.

We talked until 7:00 p.m., mostly about the domestic courts in China.

After dinner, Danru and I went to Röling's room for a visit of half an hour, because Röling had bought an oriental embroidered picture of Guanyin Bodhisattva and asked me repeatedly "to invite Gen. Wang to appreciate it."

Leaving his room, we went to the small theater to see a movie. However, I came out after just a few minutes as I was not in a good mood.

When I opened my door, Zhu Gongliang, Li Jizhi, Zhang Fengju and Xiang Mingsi had already taken seats in my room. They had also called on the waitress to make Japanese tea, over which we chatted until 10 o'clock. They then went back to the former residence of the Minister of Agriculture and Forestry, which is now the office and accommodation of the Chinese Delegation.

I practiced Tai-Chi and took a short break. At 11:00 p.m., I went to bed as there would be a judges' conference tomorrow morning, for which I would get up early.

April 10, 1946, Wednesday

Secretary Fang came at 9 o'clock in the morning, and we took the car to the courthouse. I took particular notice of the local residents' movements and facial expressions, as it was the day of the first general election in Japan's history. But I was disappointed to find that people seemed to be quiet and cheerless everywhere, definitely not as feverish as what I saw in the United States twenty years ago. I guess that the notion of election and its advantages might be a bit inexplicable for Japan's general public who had long been nurtured by fascism.

The judges' conference began at 10:00 a.m. It was chaired by the acting president Northcroft, who reported that the Tribunal had received a letter from Chief Prosecutor Keenan, saying that the Indictment was to be put forward on April 15, and that he hoped the bench to designate a date for its acceptance. This came to our surprise as no one had expected Keenan to have this plan up his sleeve. But in my mind, I still suspected that this could end up being an "empty promise," as to my knowledge, the IPS was so exhausted from overwork that they might not be able to deliver the Indictment on April 15.

However, since Mr. Keenan had thrown down the "gauntlet," we could do nothing but pick it up. We resolved to invite him here to file the Indictment on April 15, and to distribute a copy to each accused war criminal on the same day. Meanwhile, we would set another date (probably the third or fourth day after the filing) for the opening ceremony of the public prosecution, where the Indictment would be read out by the prosecutor and all the defendants would be present to plead "guilty" or "not guilty," i.e., the "arraignment." The court hearing would not begin until about a month after, so as to give the defendants and their lawyers enough time to prepare for their defense.

I proposed that copies of the Indictment accepted on April 15 should be delivered to the defendants by the Tribunal instead of the IPS. They all agreed.

So it was decided that Northcroft should discuss the details with Keenan this afternoon.

We all felt greatly relieved as the machine was finally started.

McDougall and Röling were so eager that they proposed to discuss the second draft of the Rules of Procedure. But Northcroft opposed it firmly, because Sir William Webb had not yet come back. After the meeting, I came across Col. Hanney, the director of administration, and took the opportunity to complain that the Secretariat had often spelt my name wrongly. He apologized and promised never to repeat such mistake. It was, of course, not a big deal, but he did take it seriously.

I had a cup of tea with Higgins at the bar in the building. Having similar tastes and neither of us being fond of alcohol, Higgins and I had a very cordial and pleasant talk, which seemed to symbolize the long-lasting friendship between China and the United States. He is about fifteen years older than me, so he considers himself to be an elder brother, and sometimes even call me as well as Röling "little bro."

Walking out of the bar, we returned to the hotel for lunch in the same car.

It was 3:00 p.m. when I woke up from a nap. I invited Secretary Fang to ride with me to Ueno Tōshōgū in Ueno Park. Ueno Tōshōgū used to be part of the imperial palace, but has been converted to a public museum at the instruction of the GHO, so anybody can come to visit it. Displayed there were the cultural relics such as the clothes, utensils and other belongings of Japan's past dynasties, but not in great number. We couldn't help feeling that the museum was "beautifully decorated but poorly filled." I heard that most of the fine objects had been moved elsewhere.

After visiting the museum, we went to China's Liaison Office to see the dispatches of the past few days from the Chinese Central News Agency. From cover to cover, there was almost nothing else but news about the KMT and the CPC fighting for Northeast China, and the sky-rocketing prices on the market.

From 5 to 7 o'clock in the afternoon, Fang and I perused the second draft of the Rules of Procedure prepared by Webb. We read it aloud and studied it item by item, with reference to the personal opinions raised by Col. Ollivetti (a famous legal practitioner in the Eighth Army in charge of the trials of war criminals). We found that quite some wordings in the draft were yet to be reconsidered and that, after carefully studying it once or twice more, I might be able to submit some written comments to the judges' conference, or at least I would be fully prepared for the next meeting and discussion.

All my colleagues sent by different countries are experienced and prestigious senior judges, so I have to work extremely conscientiously and sincerely, never be sloppy.

Danru invited his Japanese teacher for dinner at 8 o'clock, and he asked me to accompany them. We had a pleasant talk over dinner. Before long, Mingsi came and we talked until 11:00 p.m. I came back to my room, played Tai-Chi, took a shower, and go to bed at midnight.

April 11, 1946, Thursday

I did not go out in the morning, but just read some newspapers and wrote in my diary in the room.

I browsed *Stars and Stripes* and found a piece of news on "the indictment being delayed," as was expected, for the reason that the judge from the Soviet Union had not arrived. In fact, there should be other reasons, too. It was really an "empty promise" by the IPS as I anticipated yesterday.

The news from China was still awful with the fight for Northeast China becoming white-hot. I do miss Wanru's eldest brother Jingxuan and my younger brother Ruxuan in Changchun. They might have retreated from there, I hope! The three-person mediation team was in operation, but I'm afraid it would have no effect. It was said that Gen. Marshall would come back to China this week. How inexcusable it is to allow our own domestic affairs to be interfered by foreigners! Worse still, the economy is collapsing at the same time: the price of coal in Shanghai has surged as high as *fabi* 450,000 per ton, and one egg, according to Fang, costs 1000. What a mess it has become!

Nippon Times published a short article titled "Chinese Not Taking Revenge," describing how generous the Chinese were toward the Japanese after Japan's surrender, even to the extent that they "took the enemy as friends." Generosity, of course, is a virtue; indulgence and fear, however, is nothing but cowardice. I found the article both funny and annoying.

Mr. Keenan called, saying that Gen. MacArthur was asking if I would have time for lunch with him tomorrow. I knew it was just a courtesy question. Since we the judges were all sick of doing nothing, how could I not have time to accept Gen. MacArthur's invitation?

He asked me whether I would like to go together with him; if so, I should wait in the Imperial Hotel for him to pick me up at 1:00 p.m. I said yes.

My mustache was a little too long and I was not used to cutting it myself. So I had to go to the barber's downstairs to have it trimmed.

I ran into Röling when coming back upstairs. He insisted that we should sit for a while on the meadow beside the pond (inside the hotel yard), where he ordered two cups of coffee. He expressed great interest in and admiration for Chinese philosophy and culture. Being a man fond of learning, he seems unrestrained, outgoing and sincere, with a touch of young celebrity. His words may not be untrue.

Later, we came to the discussion on whether in the Tribunal's judgement, the number and names of the judges for it and those against it should be specified, like in the Anglo-American courts, and whether those against it should be allowed to issue their dissenting opinions. He resolutely opposed to this method, and elaborated in terms of general principles. I basically agreed with him, but said that I had yet to think it through. I told him that it was such an important matter that it should be stipulated in the Rules, or at least be discussed thoroughly in a meeting of the judges.

While Röling and I were indulged in an interesting discussion, McDougall came over to tell us that he was holding a cocktail party in his room and that we should join the others immediately. Present there were about eight or nine people, including a couple of staff members of the Tribunal apart from the judges. Higgins and I did not enjoy drinking, so we sneaked out to have lunch at the dining room.

After taking a nap, I paid a visit at 3 o'clock to Gen. Zhu at the former residence of the Minister of Agriculture and Forestry. Mr. Li, Mr. Zhang and Secretary Qian were also there, and they led me to visit the different rooms and decorations. It is a Japanese aristocratic house, with bright windows and tidy tables giving it a unique appearance. The gardens and pavilions, and the flowers and plants, are extremely neat and lovely. Seated on the ground, we sipped our tea and talked about this and that, feeling somewhat the spirit of Orientalism.

At about 4:00 p.m., a commander of the US Air Transportation Service came to visit Gen. Zhu, who invited all of us to a drink in his refined and novel parlor.

The commander (whose name I forgot) was familiar and sympathetic with the situation in China. He had traveled to Peking, Shanghai and other cities, and made a lot of Chinese friends. His brother-in-law is right now serving as the Naval Attache at the US Embassy in Chungking. He said that the Japanese were most distasteful to him as they were cunning and knavish, from his experience fighting and residing in Japan. He complained that the Japanese stole everything and became all the more audacious over time. He also said that, if the Chinese army should arrive here, he would rather move to the Chinese zone of occupation. He expressed strong dissatisfaction with America's lenient policy, which resulted in a dramatic change of attitude on the part of the Japanese: at the beginning of the occupation, they were panic-stricken and appeared as dumb as a piece of wood; later they became reverent and respectful, looking tame and pitiable; but now they were happy and content, even a little arrogant. Gen. Zhu also shared this observation.

I left alone at 6 o'clock as it was time for another party held by Lord Patrick, which McDougall, Röling, Higgins, Northcroft and Bernard all attended. Conversations with these colleagues who met with each other for at least three times a day were obviously free and hearty. But again, Higgins and I were not interested in drinking, so we left quietly to have dinner first.

After dinner, I went with Danru to see a song and dance show and a movie at the Pyle Theater. It was said that the performing troupe was not bad and had attracted a large audience. But still, there were only the two of us in the "generals' box" tonight. It was too hot in the theater, so we came back without finishing the show. I took a shower and did not go to bed until nearly midnight.

April 12, 1946, Friday

As Gen. MacArthur invited me to lunch today, I went to the courthouse with Secretary Fang early enough, so that I could return to the hotel in time to be picked up by Mr. Keenan.

Once more, we carefully studied the second draft of the Rules of Procedure item by item, and considered again the comments of Mr. Ollivetti in detail. I made some marks on the draft to prepare for the discussion at the next meeting. Having finished this work, McDougall took me to the bar where Higgins, Patrick and Röling were chatting. We all felt impatient at President Webb's long absence and the Soviet judge's delay in coming, as well as the postponement of the already scheduled Indictment filing.

Mr. Keenan came after I took a short break in the hotel. He asked the French judge Bernard and me to ride with him in his car. Mingsi, along with the prosecutors from France, the Netherlands and the Philippines, took another car. I asked my driver to follow us. We headed straight for the official residency of Gen. MacArthur in the American Embassy, and arrived there at around 1:00 p.m.

As Gen. MacArthur was still at work, we were received by his wife and a young aide.

Mrs. MacArthur is slight of figure, but is gifted with a silver tongue. Full of wit and eloquence, she offered warm hospitality to us. She expressed admiration for Chinese cultural relics, and paid tribute to President Chiang as the Chinese leader and his wife Madam Chiang. She suddenly realized that her conversation focused too much on China, so she soon switched to the beauty of Paris, the situation in the Hague, and the memories of Islas Filipinas, singing praises and making inquiries alternately. All in all, she was a good conversationalist, talkative in a graceful manner so that no one would get bored. With someone like Mrs. MacArthur in a party, the guests would never feel lonesome.

We chatted and jested for about half an hour before Gen. MacArthur came back from the GHQ.

When he entered the room, Mrs. MacArthur ran to him and gave him a hug and a kiss, which is common in Western etiquette. Then Mr. Keenan introduced us to Gen. MacArthur one by one, and we shook hands with him. After we sat down, Gen. MacArthur said sorry for being late, and suggested that we should eat and talk in the dining room.

Gen. MacArthur is strong but not heavy—a typical American soldier's figure—tall but not fat, burly but not corpulent. His bright and piercing eyes were the most charming part, making anyone whom he talked to or shook hands with feel his infinite cordiality and attraction.

I was seated on the right-hand side of Gen. MacArthur which, according to the Western customs, was the seat for the guest of honor. As we sat closer, we chatted more. He expressed diplomatically his strong interest in and profound respect for China, and also called himself an admirer of the top leader of China.

He was really in high spirits, talking in a flow of eloquence, on and on without stopping.

He was discontented with the state of affairs in the international community, which was permeated with suspicion and conflicts. He said that after World War I, the nations managed to act politely and amicably to each other; they convened a peace conference and signed a peace treaty, while the winning countries stayed in peace and harmony for a good number of years. But following this recent War, the international relations became tense almost immediately, as if the nations could not afford to take a moment to breathe, but had to move forward toward a third world war.

He brightened up with excitement and gesticulated when it came to the possibility of a third world war. He said that such a war must not happen as it would equal the extermination of the human race. From now on, a war would no longer be about who would win and who would lose, but about whether we were all willing to perish together.

He further elaborated that the invention of atomic bombs had changed the whole strategic and tactical approaches, and even the very meaning of war. Countries without such weapon could not enter the war, while those having it and participating in the war could destroy the enemy state, and be destroyed by the enemy state at the same time. As a result, everybody was doomed.

He made an in-depth research on the potency of atom bombs. Those made nowadays, he said, were much more powerful than the two used in Hiroshima and Nagasaki, with one small bomb being equal to 2000 Flying Fortresses. He also said that only 60 atomic bombs could paralyze or even wipe out the vast country of the United States, not to mention small countries. Nevertheless, even the atomic bomb marked just a starting point for newer weapons, as something more potent would definitely be invented, or perhaps had already been invented.

"Under these circumstances, how could one fight and who could win?" asked Gen. MacArthur with a smile. He then sighed, "Since there exist ambitious countries which maintain permanent armed forces of 6 million soldiers, how can we not be prepared for war?" "I am still on my guard although I am aware of the danger of war."

The French judge asked him if he knew Gen. De Gaulle. He responded that he had not met Gen. De Gaule but respected him a lot, as Gen. De Gaulle was "a most undiplomatic person" just like himself. Ah, for Christ's sake! Not only is Gen. MacArthur good at diplomacy, but he is also well qualified for the diplomatic handling of political affairs. Otherwise, how could he hold such an important post and perform his duties with such skills and ease!

He expressed his pride in the recent election in Japan and the draft constitution, which he deemed as the initial step toward democracy. I could make no comment on that.

As to Gen. MacArthur's policy on ruling Japan, I am yet to draw a conclusion as to whether its merits or demerits prevail, and whether it is more beneficial or harmful to China.

Regarding China's contribution to World War II, it seemed that Gen. MacArthur was not forgetful (unfortunately, most Anglo-Americans have banished from their minds our achievements in the fierce battles against Japanese invaders for more than eight years). He expressed his heartfelt thanks to China's collaboration with and support for the United States in the Far Eastern Commission and the Allied Council for Japan, implying satisfaction with Gen. Zhu's impartiality.

Gen. MacArthur praised China for the generously tolerant and lenient attitude of her government and people toward Japan, saying, "China is a nation of philosophy. The Chinese people are most sensible as they know that they will have to coexist peacefully with Japan in the long run."

From Gen. MacArthur's standpoint, such attitude is of course most suitable and badly needed. However, we should be vigilant while being lenient. We should heighten our vigilance toward Japan! I couldn't help recalling the article of March 29 by Mr. Lattimore.

We talked for nearly two hours, covering a big variety of topics which I cannot fully remember. Since I sat at the guest of honor's seat, I should be the first one to take leave. He saw me off at the door with his wife, and gave me a handshake as powerful as the one when we met.

Gen. MacArthur gave me the impression of being not only a military genius but also a great statesman. However, what I am most concerned about is whether his policy is detrimental to the national interests or hindering the development of my country—this problem has been hovering in my mind all day today.

I came back to the hotel at about 3:00 p.m. After a nap, I wrote three letters to my families, which I planned to give to the IPS for being taken to Shanghai by their flight tomorrow.

I talked at leisure with Patrick, Higgins, McDougall and Röling around dinner time. We all brightened up with joy when mentioning that both Sir William Webb and the Soviet judge might arrive tomorrow, as in this way, the machine could perhaps be really started at last.

I came back to my room at 9:30 and wrote in my diary, when Danru and Mingsi came to visit. I went to bed at midnight.

April 13, 1946, Saturday

I woke up and opened the newspapers, only to find bad news about China again—turf battle for Changchun was imminent. That made me miss so much my brother-in-law Jingxuan, who serves as Director of Jilin Provincial Postal Administration in Changchun, and my youngest brother Ruxuan, who works there for the Central Bank of China. I wish both of them safe and sound! And I wish all the more for peace and unity in my motherland as soon as possible!

The result of Japan's election was published. Among the elected members of the Diet, there are 139 from the Liberal Party, 92 from the Social Democratic Party, 91 from the Japan Progressive Party, 16 from the Collaboration Party, 5 from the Communist Party, 83 nonparty personages, and 38 from all the other small parties, totaling 464. Gen. MacArthur was informed of the tentative result yesterday morning. He was satisfied for the following reasons: First of all, 73% of the eligible voters participated in the election, a percentage higher than that of any other country's elections; secondly, only five of the Communist Party candidates were elected; thirdly, although it was the first time that Japanese women had gained the right to vote, as many as 38 women were elected to the Diet. He also said that the background information of all the candidates went through scrutiny; their works, speeches, behavior and experience since the year of the Mukden Incident (September 18, 1931) were all put in a form and duly reported.

Satisfied as Gen. MacArthur was—in fact he had to be so—today's news was that the press in the Soviet Union and the United Kingdom were all criticizing him, saying that it was not the right time for a general election, so it could not lead to a good outcome. On the other hand, China, while being one of the four big powers for the Far East, was too much preoccupied with the civil war and a thousand other things yet to be undertaken, and therefore failed to take notice of such an event. It had to play deaf and dumb without making any comment on it.

The previously said flight to Shanghai by the IPS' chartered plane seemed unlikely to happen soon. Around 9:00 a.m., Secretary Fang called to tell me that a Mr. Bao of the Food Section of the GHQ was going back to China tonight. So I wrote a few more letters for him to take to China.

Gen. Zhu came at noontime. We had lunch served in my room and talked until 3:00 p.m. We planned to go for a Sunday outing in Kamakura and Hayama.

I had dinner with Danru, after which we sat for a while in the Pyle Theater. There were as many as five or six people sitting in the "generals' box" tonight. The heat there drove us out after just a few minutes. We went to my room, where Mingsi joined us later. All sorts of feelings welled up in our minds as we talked about the state affairs in China. There were Japanese song and dance performance with loud music downstairs, but we were not in the mood to watch it.

After they left, I wrote in my diary and played Tai-Chi until 1:00 a.m., when I went to sleep.

April 14, 1946, Sunday

I got up late this morning and came across Röling and McDougall while taking a walk in the garden. We chatted for half an hour, and they told me that Justice Zaryanov, the judge from the Soviet Union, had arrived yesterday evening, bringing along a team of 44 members; also arrived were the Soviet prosecutors. It looked likely that the machine could be started soon. We talked about the order of the bench seats and whether the judges should take an oath as well as the issue of confidentiality.

I read the newspapers and a book for an hour or so before Secretary Fang came in and discussed whether he could take a trip back to China. I agreed in principle but could not decide on a date right now.

We had an early lunch and went to Gen. Zhu's residence, as we had agreed to gather at 1:00 p.m. and go to Kamakura.

Sitting down for a short while, I asked Secretary Qian (Gen. Zhu's confidential secretary, very familiar with Japan) what he thought about the general election in Japan. He responded that, of the more than 400 elected members, most were flunkies of warlords and financiers as well as political speculators. They could easily fool the Americans by putting on their camouflage and a mask of democracy—the Americans were so naive as to fall into their trap. This observation was totally in line with what Col. Tang had told me a few days ago.

Gen. Zhu said that the second group of his delegation, taking a chartered plane flown by the Chinese, was to arrive at nightfall. Therefore, his car would be used to pick them up at Atsugi Airport, while he rode with me in my car for Kamakura.

About two hours later, we arrived at Kamakura. We did not get off the car as the roads were unfamiliar, but only took a joy ride in downtown Kamakura and along the seashore, before telling my driver to go to Hayama. We asked for directions along the way, passed through several tunnels and a small town called "Zushi," and finally reached Hayama. Hayama is also a small town, but Japanese small towns and villages are different from those in China. First, they have electric lights, telephones and convenient transportation everywhere, showing a high level of industrialization. Secondly, houses in the country are often scattered, with frailish doors, windows and fences, not like the houses in China that have high walls and thick doors bolted and locked. This reflects that the Japanese have been living in an environment where public security is not a problem, in contrast with that in China: we have to guard our homes vigilantly, not only in the years of wars and robberies, but even in times of peace and prosperity. In my view, China's politics have been passive all the time in that, as long as no one rebels against the imperial court (government), it is considered a perfect world; as to people's livelihood, education, hygiene, etc., those can only be left to God's mercy and the people's own fate. Hoping that the weather is good and the people happy, the Chinese government will do or care for nothing at all.

By the seashore of Hayama we saw a fort belonging to Yokosuka, with an old sign forbidding entrance which had been put up by Japan's Ministry of War. But now it is open to anybody who comes to visit and ponder on the past.

We took a walk by the seashore for a while before going home. When we passed by the US Cavalry Brigade Command in Yokosuka, the four American guards raised their guns as a salute to show respect for us the moment they saw the Chinese national emblem on my car. It was natural and convenient for Gen. Zhu to return it with a military salute. As I was in civilian clothes, should I wave my hand, or take off my hat, or rather nod my head to them? This has puzzled me a lot for days and sometimes makes me feel embarrassed. I will have to make a study on it.

Having passed Zushi, we came to Yokohama, but the driver took a wrong turn. The road was very bumpy and we were sitting in the car like dancing, even much worse than the road from Beipei to Qingmuguan in Chungking that I used to tread in the past eight years. Gen. Zhu said that the Japanese roads were in bad condition, and most country roads were just like this one.

Alas, this made me realize and understand something.

The Japanese are so good at putting up a facade and conducting false propaganda. They always recommend to others that they should visit here and there, by describing many metropolis and scenic spots as paradise or an Eastern nirvana. They publish exaggerated guidebooks, tourist series and similar books and newspapers, hold art exhibitions, concerts and Kabuki, as well as select beautiful girls to serve at various restaurants and hotels. Who can be sure that these intoxicating and tempting things do not contain the poisonous element of cheating? But the Westerners, American youngsters in particular, are easily fooled. Japan's strategy of promoting itself has been successful both before and after the War, and it is not easy for outsiders to find out the truth. I would never know how poor a Japanese road could get, should we not have taken the wrong turn, and how poor the country roads in general were, should Gen. Zhu not have told us so.

It was not until nearly 7:00 p.m. that we returned to the place of our delegation. The plane from China had not arrived yet, so I dined with Gongliang first. We were soon interrupted by a phone call from Danru, who told us that the Chinese plane did not even take off from Shanghai today, and it had been rescheduled for tomorrow. I said goodbye to Gongliang and came to the hotel at 8:40, right in time for a movie named *The Dolly Sisters.* It was a song and dance drama in color, with simple plot but lively scenes, representing a common genre of American movies.

After the movie, Danru and Mingsi talked with me for about an hour in my room. Then I wrote in my diary, played Tai-Chi and took a shower. Again, I did not go to bed until 1:00 a.m.

April 15, 1946, Monday

Today is the first wedding anniversary for Wanru and me. However, I even have no idea where she is now. Maybe she has left Chungking and is on her way to Shanghai, or maybe she has already arrived in Shanghai. Transportation in China is so difficult, which makes me miss her very badly. I keep recalling memories of this day a year ago. I can do nothing but wish for her health and a safe and smooth journey on the Yangtze River (Fig. 1).

The weather was very warm, and the cherries blossomed everywhere. The scene at the Imperial Hotel reminded me of last year today in Shufan Mansion in the North Hot Springs in Chungking.

At the beginning of this month when I wrote to Wanru and asked Dr. Gu to bring a small gift to her, I told her that I would host a dinner party on April 15 for sure.

When I woke up in the morning, I was wondering whom to invite and which cuisine to offer: Chinese, Japanese or Western? All of a sudden, Danru came with an invitation card in his hand—it was from the Overseas Chinese Federation in Japan, for the purpose of welcoming Gen. Zhu and me to Tokyo. I believe it was mainly in Gen. Zhu's honor, as he was their officer in charge, while I would only be an accompanying guest. Besides, a large number of the Chinese Delegation members would arrive in Tokyo this evening, so both Gongliang and Danru would also be greeting those new members. In this case, I had no choice but to give up the idea of hosting a party. Fortunately, a grand gathering like this one with the Overseas Chinese Federation would be way better than my small party in a group of four or five. I would just take advantage of this gathering to celebrate my own anniversary, since I was compelled by the force of circumstances.

Fig. 1 Mei Ju-ao and his wife Wanru (Xiao Kan)

In the morning, I still went to the courthouse with Secretary Fang to handle some official business, and chatted with McDougall and Röling for a while. They told me that Gen. Zaryanov from the Soviet Union had arrived, and they had dinner with him yesterday evening. He could not speak even a word of English, and the young major colonel who translated for him was not so good, either. It could be a problem for the future meetings and trial sessions.

I received a phone call from Gongliang, who said that the event to be held by the Overseas Chinese Federation was a tea party, and there would be many people attending it. He asked me to join him at 3:30 p.m. to go to the party together.

I took a nap after lunch and came to Gongliang's office on time, where three overseas Chinese representatives were already waiting there to welcome us.

About seven or eight attendees went with us, so we took four cars. Gen. Zhu, Secretary Fang and I rode in the same car, which reached at about 4 o'clock the Chinese restaurant in Ueno Park, the largest Chinese restaurant in Tokyo. By the time we arrived, there had already been several hundred overseas Chinese standing around. I learned later that tomorrow would be the annual conference of the Overseas Chinese Federation, for which reason there were many representatives coming from all over Japan to Tokyo today, and they took this opportunity to hold a party for Gen. Zhu.

Several overseas Chinese leaders greeted us in the parlor, before everybody entered the auditorium for a meeting. The auditorium was not small but was very crowded with people. The cigarettes, alcoholic drinks and snacks were all Japanese local products, which had a distinctive flavor. I had some dried fish but dared not to smoke the Japanese cigarette, as in my experience, even the best brand was inferior to the worst ones made in Chungking.

Mr. Zhou, President of the Overseas Chinese Federation, made an opening speech, and then asked Gen. Zhu to give an "admonitory talk," which was translated into Taiwanese by Mr. Xie Nanguang. Gen. Zhu's speech was pretty long and stern. Afterwards I asked about the inside story and was told that among those many Chinese living in Japan, there were bad as well as good ones. Although most of them led an honest life, quite a number of them made troubles and did all sorts of evils. Some had acted suspiciously during the Japanese aggression against China, while some were even still colluding with local ruffians and engaging in black market transactions and other disreputable affairs. That was the reason why Gen. Zhu made the speech not only to encourage the good behavior but also to reprimand and warn the bad elements.

The president asked me to say a few words after Gen. Zhu's speech, to my surprise. I hesitated for a while but, not in a position to refuse him, I tried my best to talk for about ten to fifteen minutes, with Mr. Xie translating into Taiwanese paragraph by paragraph.

I only put forward two wishes. First, I wish all the overseas Chinese to pay attention to their own words and deeds and maintain the demeanor of the people from a great country, so as to match up to China's high international status that we have managed to achieve. Secondly, I wish all of them to be united, not divided, and resolve things in a democratic way. When there appears an issue, we should fully discuss and allow all different opinions to be freely expressed; however, once a public vote has been cast, all of us must obey the majority and abide by it, and nobody should bring up objections or cause extra complications. This was the most common weak point that I observed among the overseas Chinese twenty years ago in America and subsequently in Europe; in other words, the overseas Chinese in a country were often divided rather than united together. I thought it might be a good occasion for me to elaborate on it, especially in light of tomorrow's annual conference of the Overseas Chinese Federation in Japan.

There was a brief discussion after my speech. Gen. Zhu and I made our farewell, and the President closed the meeting.

Col. Tang and Secretary Fang came to my hotel with me and I ordered tea and snacks to my room. We chatted for an hour before they went back to their Daiichi Hotel.

When I came to the bar at about 6 o'clock, I saw there the judges from all the countries except the Soviet Union. They were drinking and talking lively and jovially. Sir William Webb, our president, had finally returned from Australia. After being introduced to each other, he and I talked earnestly for a long time as it was our first meeting. He seems about 60 years old, quite big and tall. I congratulated him on his recent promotion to the bench of the High Court (i.e., the supreme court) of Australia, from the position of chief justice in the Supreme Court of Queensland. He was pleased to hear that.

Webb was very friendly and sincere. He did not talk much, but what he said was pertinent and fair, and he looked confident in what he was doing. An elegant gentleman—that was my first impression of him.

We had dinner together and then talked in the hall. Northcroft and others told me not to call Webb "Sir," and neither would Webb call me "Doctor"; instead, we should address each other just as William or Webb, Ju-ao or Mei, etc. Although this was the first time that I had met Webb, we felt like old friends and clicked with each other.

I was eager to find out whether the new members of the Chinese Delegation had arrived, so I went upstairs as early as 9:00 p.m. I went to Danru's room and there were two from China who wanted to use his shower, so I knew that the airplane did arrive today. Later, Mingsi passed me four letters: one from my youngest brother Ruxuan in Jinzhou, one from my fifth younger sister Yunzhen in Baisha, one from Secretary Luo in Shanghai, and the last one from my dear wife Wanru in Chungking.

I was a bit disappointed that there was no letter from my father. But in the letters from Wanru and my brother and sister, I learned that my father and mother were busy preparing to return to our hometown, and both were in good health. Wanru wrote me a long letter, saying that she had received the letters which I asked Dr. Gu and Adviser Bai to send for me when they went back to China. She told me a lot about what happened in Chungking and what happened to our families, which was much to my relief. The only thing worrying me was that Wanru's eldest brother Jingxuan had not yet retreated from Changchun. She said that she would leave Chungking on April 12 by the Hongkui Ship, a special one owned by the General Post Office, but she could not arrive in Shanghai until the end of this month. It has been just four days since her departure, and she is probably in Shashi right now! I feel sorry for the miseries she has to endure due to our separation. I can do nothing but wish her a happy journey, safe and sound.

What happened today was quite a coincidence which thrilled me a lot.

I missed Wanru so much on this very first anniversary—April 15. And it was right on this day that I received her first letter from China. What's more amazing was that, while I was going to host a small party to celebrate it, all the overseas Chinese here gave a grand welcome party today, with warmth and liveliness not second to that in Shufan Mansion on this day of last year!

With such a fortuitous coincidence, I felt extremely satisfied. Today I was wearing the white shirt and red tie which I wore on the wedding day a year ago. I admit that I was a bit childish to care about such trivia. But as Mencius said, "The great man is he who does not lose his child's heart." I may have exaggerated on it, though.

I came back to my room and read again those letters and the enclosed Chinese newspaper reports on me. I wrote in my diary and played Tai-Chi before going to bed after 1:00 a.m.

April 16, 1946, Tuesday

Before noon I went to the courthouse as usual to check on some office matters, none of which were very important. I tried on the judge's robe prepared by the Tribunal (an imitation of the Anglo-Australian style) and chatted with McDougall, Röling and Higgins for half an hour at the bar.

From there I went to the Chinese Delegation at the former residence of the Minister of Agriculture and Forestry, to visit some members who had arrived last night. Shen Jinding, the chief adviser, and Lin Dingping, former deputy chief of the Foreign Ministry's Department of East Asian Affairs, were my old acquaintances, whom I invited to lunch at the Imperial Hotel so as to have a happy get-together. I talked about some recent situation in China, and we could not help uttering a heavy sigh. Our international status has been elevated substantially due to our huge sacrifice in the eight years' bloody war, but if we do not live up to the expectations, this hard-earned status will soon decline.

Messrs. Shen and Lin left after lunch. I took a nap for an hour, and then started to write to Wanru, my father, and my younger brother and sister, because the plane to China would depart either tomorrow or the day after. In the evening, I continued to write except for a 30-minute chat with Webb and Northcroft after dinner.

Mingsi came to talk at 10:00 p.m. He had a tremendously difficult task because, with the Indictment being close to completion, information collected for the part on China was still insufficient, and the translation work faced a shortage of manpower as well. (I had recently asked Secretary Fang to help him as much as possible, but since Secretary Liu was ill, it was still not enough.) Meanwhile, he was being pushed to move out of this hotel, which upset him even more. Much as I am sympathetic to his situation, I am unable to render assistance as judges cannot cooperate with prosecutors—in Britain and the US, even any contact between them must be avoided.

I have told the other judges that China would not disallow communications between the judge and the prosecutor, and that Mingsi staying at the Imperial Hotel should not be a problem. However, since the Tribunal is organized in an Anglo-American style and has essentially adopted the common law procedures, it will not be appropriate for us to argue for a different approach. Nevertheless, the GHQ seems to have treated the prosecutors unfairly this time. Except for the Chief Prosecutor Keenan, who is blowing his own trumpet and making a hit, the prosecutors from the other countries appear obscure and unknown, acting like his mere assistants. The names of the nine judges from different countries have often been mentioned in newspapers and sometimes highly praised; each stays in a three-room suite at the Imperial Hotel and has his own black car with a national flag painted on it. On the other hand, the prosecutors have not been received properly by the GHQ, which has not even designated a hotel for them to stay in. This is really unreasonable. No wonder Mingsi was full of complaints.

We kept talking until after midnight. I wrote in my diary, played Tai-Chi and went to bed at nearly 1:00 a.m.

April 17, 1946, Wednesday

It rained heavily today. Most of the days were sunny since I came to Tokyo, and it was rare to have a pouring and continuous rain like this.

Since the plane to China will take off tomorrow and there was not much to do in the Tribunal's office, I wrote letters in my room all day long amid the depressing weather. Apart from the letters I had written to my father, Boping, Wanru, Uncle Yangchun, Brother Ruxuan and Sister Yunzhen, I also wrote to my friends including Hu Jichun, Liu Shifang, Ye Qiuyuan, Li Gufan, Ren Jiafeng, Luo Jiyi, Quan Zenggu and Zhang Mingyang, as well as another two letters to my brother-in-law Jiefu and sister-in-law Wenru. Together with the previously written letters that I had tried in vain for several times to entrust the IPS for mailing, there would be some twenty letters, I'm afraid, which I hope could indeed be taken to Shanghai by the Chinese plane tomorrow.

I put all the letters into properly addressed envelopes and took them in person to Gen. Zhu in the afternoon. I seriously urged Secretary Qian Gechuan to hand them to the pilot and request him to mail them immediately upon his arrival in Shanghai.

After dinner, Danru came to visit me with a Mr. Fu. We had a drink in a Japanese pub, but I was not very interested and soon went out to the Daiichi Hotel to talk to Col. Tang, Secretary Fang and Mr. Liu, a representative of our Ministry of Foreign Affairs who would return to China tomorrow. I asked Mr. Liu to pass a small package to Wanru c/o Boping.

Coming back to the hotel, I ran into Higgins. He asked me to have a cup of coffee together and informed me that since Webb had come back from his leave, there were many issues to discuss, one of them being the seating arrangement of the bench. He held that it should follow the order of the signatory countries on Japan's Instrument of Surrender. Webb seemed to agree with this in principle, but for the convenience of the actual work, the seat for China and that for the UK might be switched, and those for France, Canada and Holland might also be changed. In fact, I have pondered for a long time over this matter, which is also a matter of concern for all. McDougall talked with me about it as early as the second day of my arrival in Tokyo. Fortunately, the outcome would be clear through the judges' conference tomorrow, so I have to take it coolly for the time being.

I returned to my room, played Tai-Chi and took a shower. It was around midnight when I went to bed.

[April 19, 1946, Friday]

[Here, several pages are missing from the original diary, and the following is deemed to be the latter part of the entry for April 19, 1946. —Editor's note]

... [At the rehearsal,] the journalists' section was crowded with people, some of whom came to test for the audio effect and short-handwriting, but most were photographers and film shooters. They were "shooting" us relentlessly from different angles and in different positions, from the moment we walked onto the platform until we stepped down, making me feel like being in a battle front. Today's rehearsal was probably held for them, and it was indeed said so, as on the day when the Tribunal was officially opened, they might not have a chance to approach and "shoot" the judges so closely, and also their attention might have to be diffused to the defendants, lawyers and guests. Therefore, they should prepare some shots of the judges in advance, for which today was their golden opportunity.

Apart from photo-taking, we also tested the audio system and the efficiency of interpretation, the results being satisfactory in general. I felt that everything in the courtroom could be carried on unimpededly even without use of the microphone.

After a short break in the conference room, the nine of us were led to the steps in the middle of the front door to have our "official photographs" taken. Again, we put on our robes and stood in two rows, with five in front and four behind. I stood in the front row between the President and the Soviet judge. In the extremely dazzling sunshine, we were put at mercy of the photographers, posing and being shot by them for about twenty minutes. They took countless pictures to their full satisfaction. Shortly after, I saw them working on our cars and drivers by arraying them and shooting many more photos. How playful the American youngsters were to "Hollywoodize" almost everything.

Back in the hotel, I came across Danru and Mr. Yun Zhen, adviser and head of the Second Group of the Chinese Delegation who had recently arrived in Japan. I invited them to have lunch with me in my room.

I read *War Criminals: Their Prosecution and Punishment* by Glueck from 3 to 6 o'clock in the afternoon. This was not a lengthy book, but I read it off and on, and had almost forgotten it recently. What a shame!

I chatted with my colleagues before dinner in the bar. After having dinner together, Higgins and Röling asked me to continue talking with them in the corridor. We discussed political issues which we had seldom mentioned before. Higgins made a lot of complaints. He looks down upon Roosevelt (saying that he was tricked by Churchill), and he is anti-British as he is a descendant of the Irish. He said that he always had a deep love for China, and that the one nation which Americans in general felt most friendly with was the Chinese. What he said was not a hypocritical expression, which in my view is by and large the true fact. Nonetheless, we must live up to the expectations, as otherwise we will only "gladden our enemies and aggrieve our friends."

Mingsi came for a talk before I went to sleep. He said that the Indictment was almost ready, and that he planned to move out of the Imperial Hotel tomorrow. He has been very busy, tired and unhappy these days (not to mention that Secretary Liu is ill again). I am really sympathetic toward him.

I played Tai-Chi after he left. It was again almost 1:00 a.m. when I went to bed. I have been staying up too late recently.

April 20, 1946, Saturday (One Month of My Arrival in Japan)

Today is my one-month commemoration day of arriving in Tokyo. Short as one month is, the past one seemed quite a long period of time to me. A few personal minor things are worth recording here.

First, I have put on weight by seven pounds since I left Shanghai. It might have something to do with the easy and comfortable life here and my simple mind for the time being.

Secondly, never in the past had I grown a mustache (except for a short time after I became ill in the spring two years ago, which I soon shaved off). It was not until I left Shanghai this time that I decided to grow it. Now it has taken shape and I have to go to the hotel barber's for a trim every week.

Thirdly, from April 1939 until recently, I did not drink cold water or cold tea, neither did I eat anything sweet before meal. But all these taboos have been broken now. I drink cold water and eat ice-cream whenever and wherever I want, and care no more whether the food I am taking is savory or sweet, hot or cold. I seem to have completely restored my unperturbed and careless spirit when I lived abroad between the ages of 20 and 25.

Finally, having played Tai-Chi in the past two years, I have continued to practice it as well as some other exercises once a day without interruption since I came to Japan. This is something more or less satisfactory.

I went to the courthouse with Secretary Fang in the morning. On the way I saw McDougall, Patrick, Northcroft and Röling, who were going to play golf in the suburb. After reviewing a few papers in the office, I asked Higgins to have a cup of coffee in the bar, where we chatted for half an hour. We did not see Bernard from France and Zaryanov from the Soviet Union, who were probably not here. Speaking of Zaryanov, he was often alone, appearing and disappearing unexpectedly, and rarely hung around with these colleagues.

Leaving the Tribunal, I went to the Chinese Delegation at the former residence of the Minister of Agriculture and Forestry. Gen. Zhu went out for business, so I talked with Gen. Wang and Secretary Qian for a while, and came back to the hotel for lunch. In the afternoon, I received a phone call from Mingsi, who decided to go back to China by the IPS chartered plane tomorrow morning. I therefore wrote two letters (one to Boping and the other to Uncle Yangchun) and prepared a box of small presents (for Wanru c/o Boping), which I would ask Mingsi to take to Shanghai.

I took a look at the bar at 7:00 p.m. and found two English gentlemen—Northcroft and Patrick—there having a drink. They insisted that I should sit down with them, and ordered for me a bottle of Coca Cola with a quarter of Rum. This is nothing to them, but I unexpectedly got drunk! In the beginning, I did not feel anything wrong as the Coco Cola tasted so good (which was my favorite drink twenty years ago in America). Little by little, my face started to burn and my heart to pound. Things got worse at dinner when I felt a bit dizzy, and the waitresses seemed to be laughing at me as well. I had to come back to my room and lie down after dinner. Though my heartbeat was fast and my head giddy, I did not throw up. I was such a "loser" in this. Other people, even Wanru, would laugh at me should they be told of this.

Mingsi came at 11:00 p.m., saying that for this trip back to China, his major task was to recruit some assistants, and also to gather supporting materials. I teased him that he would be reunited with his wife tomorrow as she had arrived in Shanghai. The last two months were exhausting for him indeed.

At 1 o'clock after midnight, I went upstairs and helped him with packing. We talked while putting together his belongings. It was 3:10 a.m. when we shook hands to say goodbye. I went to bed immediately.

April 21, 1946, Sunday

I stayed up too late last night, so I was still in a dream when Mingsi called to say goodbye. I got up at nearly 9 o'clock.

I played Tai-Chi after washing and dressing. After breakfast, Danru came and told me about Mingsi's departure from the hotel this morning. Being Sunday today, Danru did not have to go to work but asked me to take a walk in the park. It happened that my car had just arrived, so we rode in it to the Chinese Delegation. After talking with Gen. Zhu and Secretary Qian, we also paid a visit in the backyard to Mr. Zhang Fengju and Dr. Li Jizhi, the latter of whom had recently come from an investigative trip to Kyoto. As our purpose was nothing but a walk, we wandered in the garden for a long time. I also took one pot of evergreen and one of cactus to my car, which I planned to bring back to my hotel.

A mere walk around the garden did not please us to our hearts' content, while a spring day like this with gentle breeze and cherry blossom should never be wasted. As such, I invited Gongliang and Danru to a ride in my car around the splendid and imposing Chichibunomiya Mansion, which was in the style of a British palace. The roads in Tokyo were good and the appearance of the city magnificent, in this area at least, thus deserving its status as the capital of a once powerful state.

We got off at Ueno Park, where a multitude of visitors paid extra attention to us—out of a car painted with the Chinese national flag came two Chinese uniformed generals and a Chinese man with mustache, which of course aroused their curiosity. But they did not appear to be hostile or belittling, probably because they were "too busy wallowing in self-pity," or "enduring hardships to accomplish their ambitions." The Allied countries should watch out.

Apart from taking a long walk in Ueno Park, we also visited an oil-painting exhibition in an art gallery. There were many artworks, presented in more than twenty rooms. The paintings were not bad, but there seemed nothing very outstanding. It paled into insignificance in comparison with the oil-painting gallery in Paris that I visited in the spring of 1930. However, the Japanese are good at imitating. We should not underestimate their achievements in holding an exhibition like this.

It was almost 1:00 p.m. when we returned to the hotel. I invited Gen. Zhu to have lunch in my room, after which we talked about our respective trips around Europe many years ago. He left at 3 o'clock.

I stayed up too late last night, so I caught up on sleep for two or three hours.

When I woke up, Zhang Renzhong, a reporter of the Chinese Central News Agency, visited me with Danru. Mr. Zhang then invited us to dinner at the Press Club. I also would like to breathe some fresh air, as the Imperial Hotel lacked youthful vigor, and I got bored with meeting with those elderly judges day in and day out.

The news reporters were active and energetic after all. How lively their dining hall was! The food was not bad, either. We sat in Mr. Zhang's room for a long time after dinner. As a man with ambition and talent (a graduate of the National Southwestern Associated University), he was one of the few war correspondents in China. We listened with great interest to his stories about landing in Japan and in Korea with the troops.

Coming back to the hotel, I wrote in my diary, played Tai-Chi and took a shower. I did not go to bed until 1:00 a.m. again, which had almost become a routine for some time now. I should sleep earlier from now on.

April 22, 1946, Monday

It was reported in the newspaper this morning that the representative of New Zealand to the Far Eastern Commission (FEC—the decision-making body of the eleven Allied Powers for Japan) expressed dissatisfaction with America's huge supply of food provisions to Japan and suggested an investigation. This was more or less a protest against Gen. MacArthur's policy. Meanwhile, MacArthur's GHQ withdrew Gen. Marquat, the US representative and acting chairman of the Allied Council for Japan composed of the four Allied Powers, and replaced him with Atcheson, the political adviser of the GHQ. Atcheson had served as counselor and chargé d'affaires in the American embassy in China for many years, and I met him once in Chungking. Last year when Ambassador Hurley resigned with rage and roar in the US, Atcheson was one of his targets accused of having leaked American military secrets and shielded the revolutionaries in Yan'an. Subsequently, Hurley failed and the US government declared Atcheson not guilty.

These two pieces of news showed that the countries relating to the Far East had overt contention and covert struggles within both organizations—the FEC in Washington DC and the Allied Council for Japan in Tokyo. It was not impossible that other countries were averse to the US monopoly and Gen. MacArthur's lenient policy toward Japan. The replacement of Marquat by Atcheson showed America's compromise with the Soviet Union. In addition, Marquat's weakness in self-control and his policy for the use of the meaningless filibuster might also have contributed to his failure.

At 10:00 a.m., the Tribunal held a judges' conference to discuss the reply from Gen. MacArthur on whether the defendants could defend themselves without using lawyers. As this reply failed to see the key to the issue, the bench decided to send another letter of inquiry. Secondly, for any document which needed translation, the meeting came to the conclusion that such translation should be delivered 24 hours before being used in court. The meeting also discussed some other matters and ended at noontime.

I slept for two hours after lunch, probably because I was too tired and slept too little in the past few days.

At 5:00 p.m., Dr. Li Jizhi came for a visit. He told me about his investigation in Kyoto on the Chinese cultural relics in Japan. Regarding the instruction of the GHQ to the Japanese government that all cultural relics plundered to Japan from other countries since 1937 (the Marco Polo Bridge Incident) must be registered within a time limit and prohibited from trafficking, Dr. Li wanted to have it expanded into a proposal and ask Gen. Zhu to put it forward to the Allied Council for Japan. I fully agreed with him and contributed a few of my own comments.

At around 6 o'clock, Secretary Fang, Secretary Liu and Gen. Wang arrived one after another. I ordered tea and snacks, and we talked to our hearts' content.

After dinner, I watched a movie in the theater, but quit after half an hour as I was bored. Coming back to my room, I wrote in my diary, played Tai-Chi, and took a shower. It was 15 minutes after midnight when I went to bed, which was earlier than before.

April 23, 1946, Tuesday

The newspapers reported that Changchun had been completely occupied by the Communist army (I am very anxious about my brother-in-law Jingxuan's safety), that the KMT's New First Army suffered heavy casualties, and that Harbin was totally surrounded by the enemy forces and was about to be abandoned. The conflicts between the KMT and the CPC were extremely fierce. Gen. Marshall seemed to have reached his wit's end, and President Chiang Kai-shek might make another concession. Another piece of news was that the government decided to return to Nanking as China's capital again by the coming May 1, from then on all correspondence should be sent to Nanking. It will finally happen this time. But we still wonder whether the National Assembly scheduled for May 5 will be postponed due to the civil war. What an ill-starred motherland! I wish her to turn calamities into blessings and to bury the hatchets and make peace!

This morning, we had another judges' meeting, in which we discussed the wording and process of the oaths to be taken by judges, interpreters, recorders, reporters, and some other staff members. The proposed oath by interpreters and reporters had the phrase "So help me God," but I suggested to delete it or at least amend it in some way, as they might not be all Christians. This suggestion was accepted and the meeting decided not to use that wording to non-Christians. As for the oath by the judges, it was another set without the expression "So help me God."

In addition, we discussed some minor changes to the Rules of Procedure. As Gen. MacArthur had not replied to our letter of yesterday, we were still not clear whether there was a contradiction with the Charter.

After the meeting, Gen. Zaryanov walked to me and shook hands with me. We talked for about ten minutes. I told him that I passed through Moscow in the severe winter in February 1929. "You must be a child at that time as you now look just in your late 20's or early 30's," said he. I did not know whether he really meant it or said so only as a humorous courtesy. But anyway, a Chinese man is always deemed younger than his actual age by foreigners, maybe because of his black hair and short stature. Take Mingsi for example: he is ten years older than me, about 51 or 52, but in the eyes of Westerners, he looks like a man in his 30's. This puts us Chinese at a disadvantage. I am not sure whether my growing a mustache will be of any help to this matter.

After saying good-bye to Zaryanov with a handshake, I had a cup of coffee with McDougall and Patrick at the bar. Then I went to visit the Chinese Delegation, but Gen. Zhu was not there, so I had a chat with Group Leader Yun and Secretary Qian, and browsed through some publications received from China.

After lunch back in the hotel, I talked with Higgins in the corridor for half an hour. He told me that, regarding the judges' seating arrangement, Webb reconsidered it over again and decided to maintain the order of the signatory countries on Japan's Instrument of Surrender, so as to avoid any unexpected misunderstanding or unnecessary disputes. I expressed my total support and commendation for Webb's impartiality and clear-headedness.

I came back for a nap. From 4 to 6 o'clock in the afternoon, I read in detail *Stars and Stripes* and *Nippon Times* of the past few days, and the latest issues of *Newsweek* and *Time*. Editing techniques of foreign magazines were really advanced that I was attracted so much when reading them. Zhu Gongliang came at 6:00 p.m. We had dinner together, and went to the nearby Pyle Theater to see the famous stage play *Arsenic & Lace*. The play was about a madman's family. Two old aunts poisoned twelve people and a lunatic nephew also killed twelve. The plot was interwoven with love stories. The dialogues were good and the actors and actresses performed quite well. But the theme was too bizarre, which might be a stimulus to the American audience who were bored with a much too easy and comfortable life.

After the play, Gen. Zhu came to my room and talked for a long time, mostly about how things stood in the Allied Council for Japan and the significance of the replacement of Marquat by Atcheson. Gongliang had a penetrating insight and a sincere friendship with Atcheson. I believe that he would seize the opportunity and make good use of it.

I played Tai-Chi and wrote in my diary after he left. It was again nearly 1:00 a.m. when I went to sleep.

I played a set of Tai-Chi at 4 o'clock in the afternoon and another set before bedtime. This was the first time that I had practiced twice in a day during the past month or so since I came to Tokyo. I hope I can keep on practicing twice a day from now on. However, if I can only manage to do it once, it would be better to make it during the daytime, as to exercise just before sleeping seems not so healthy.

ACME Newspictures gave us two samples of the photos taken at the rehearsal the day before yesterday—the nine judges standing in front of the Tribunal's building. We did not look at ease as the sunshine was too dazzling. Gen. Zhu was satisfied with my posture and said that except for the Russian judge and me, all the others looked a bit elderly. I responded to him, that was the typical appearance of judges in the West!

April 24, 1946, Wednesday

We had a judges' meeting this morning, where we continued to discuss the draft Rules of Procedure and the matter of translation of the documents and records. We only made some minor revisions on the Rules and passed them as the fourth draft.

In the course of our discussion of the draft, the Secretariat passed us the reply letter from Gen. MacArthur, with a draft amendment to the Charter of the Tribunal enclosed. In answer to the question asked in our letter, the amendment prescribes that each defendant is allowed to conduct his defense either by himself or through a lawyer appointed by him, but he must choose one of these two options. The other amendment to the Charter is to increase the number of the judges, with two representatives from India and the Philippines respectively. Each of the two countries may also send to the IPS an associate prosecutor to assist the Chief Prosecutor.

After the meeting, I had lunch back in the hotel. It rained heavily, so I did not go out. Waking up from a nap, I immersed myself into letter writing as Mr. Zeng Siqing of the Central News Agency was to return to China tomorrow. I continued to write after having dinner at 7 o'clock. By 10 o'clock when Secretary Fang and Secretary Liu came to take the letters, I had finished six and handed them all to be passed to Mr. Zeng, so that he could post them upon arrival in Shanghai tomorrow.

I read the newspapers till midnight. The chaotic world was fraught with so many problems. But what concerned me most was the downfall of the Shidehara Cabinet (which resigned en bloc yesterday) and who his successor would be, as well as the situation in Northeast China. Thoughts on the thorny path to our country's future and the danger of declination of her international status made me toss and turn in bed. As a saying goes, "Lookers-on see most of the game." The latent danger may not be realized so clearly by those staying in the country as us stationed abroad.

April 25, 1946, Thursday

I read the newspapers in the morning, which reported that the National Assembly on the formation of a constitution, originally scheduled for May 5, was to be postponed as the CPC and the China Democratic League refused to designate their representatives and the Northeast issue was yet to be resolved. In the meantime, Ambassador Marshall was meditating for peace, and the government also had the intention to make another concession.

We held another judges' conference this morning and discussed the fourth draft of the Rules of Procedure. With only minor changes in the wording, this draft was basically finalized.

After discussion of the draft Rules, each judge signed our oath, as follows:

> We affirm that, as Members of the International Military Tribunal for the Far East, we will duly administer justice according to law, without fear, favor or affection, according to our conscience, and the best of our understanding, and that we will not disclose or discover the vote or opinion of any particular member of the Tribunal upon findings or sentence but will preserve inviolate the secrecy of the counsel of every member.

Our oath was signed in the following order: the United States, China, Britain, the Soviet Union, Canada, Australia, France, the Netherlands and New Zealand. I signed my name in Chinese followed by an English translation (Fig. 2).

Fig. 2 Justice Mei in his office

The signing ceremony was extremely simple with nothing special to be called as a "ceremony." After that the meeting was ended, and I returned to the hotel for lunch and a nap.

I then skimmed through several books and magazines that Danru brought me yesterday evening. At 6:00 p.m., I went to visit the Chinese Delegation and talked with its head Gen. Zhu, Adviser Shen, Group Leader Yun and Secretary Qian for an hour or so, mostly about the situation in China and the Delegation's attitude toward the successor of Japan's prime minister. Gen. Zhu said that he was against a party chieftain (Ichiro Hatoyama) who appeared to be the most likely candidate to form a cabinet, for which he had submitted a statement to the GHQ.

Therefore, Hatoyama's illusion about heading a cabinet fell through completely. It was an unprecedented entitlement for us Chinese to approve the candidacy for the prime minister of Japan! I wish our fellow countrymen to cherish our good name and unite in building up our country, so as to maintain our international status.

After dinner in the hotel, I saw a movie named *Detour* in the small theater. The protagonist was not so well-known but the plot and his acting skills were not bad.

Danru came for a visit at 11:00 p.m. I washed and slept at nearly 1:00 a.m.

April 26, 1946, Friday

It was rainy today. Originally, there was no judges' meeting scheduled for today. I asked Secretary Fang to come over to discuss the translation of the Charter and the Rules of Procedure. I asked him to retype several copies, and start revising the translation of the Charter as well as translating the Rules of Procedure as soon as possible.

Upon his arrival at the courthouse, Secretary Fang called urgently to say that Sir William Webb informed him of an unscheduled meeting at 11:30 a.m., for which I needed to go to the office at once.

The meeting was only about one simple but important matter: to designate a date and time for the acceptance of the IPS' Indictment, as Mr. Keenan sent a letter saying that the Indictment would be completed by next Monday and could then be delivered to the Tribunal at any time. We decided that all the judges would be present to accept the Indictment in the conference room at 11:00 a.m. on Monday.

Thank goodness! The long-awaited Indictment will finally be presented. The trial machine may really be started this time. I hope this is not a false alarm or empty joy. It is high time that Mr. Keenan honored his words!

I met a Miss Wang who was looking for Danru when I went back to the hotel and asked Danru to join me for lunch. The young lady's father is Chinese and her mother Portuguese. She seemed smart, vivacious, and totally childish. She was said to speak several languages and her Chinese and English were pretty good indeed. She worked for the American Red Cross. She was the first Chinese girl I had met since I came to Japan.

I took a nap after lunch. Then I went through carefully the latest revised draft of the Rules of Procedure and found it improved a lot from the previous version.

After dinner I chatted in the corridor with Higgins, McDougall and two American officers. The two officers seemed to know some facts about China, and one of them had been to Peking and Tientsin. But being well-cultivated men, they did not question or talk about the headline stories played up by the newspapers recently, such as "civil war in China," "the battle for Changchun," and "Chinese famine: Millions of people eating roots, leaves and dirt." In fact, my fellow judges have seen the bad news about China every day, but they are tight-lipped and never talk about the political situation in China, or any international affairs that may cause awkwardness. This is probably the characteristic of what is called "gentlemen." And this is an advantage of staying at the Imperial Hotel. Elsewhere, there could be a lot of less decent people, who might ask all sorts of questions that could embarrass us from China, one of the so-called "Five Big Powers." As I recall it, Commissioner Liu told me three weeks ago that when he was talking to an American junior officer about the rations for the overseas Chinese, the officer said bluntly: "The newspaper says millions of Chinese are eating grass roots and tree leaves. Then, why should the overseas Chinese have better rations than the Japanese?" After Commissioner Liu refuted him, he said: "Forget it. Let's talk about something else. Why does China still have a civil war? Let's discuss what the KMT and the CPC are fighting about, shall we?" It is really ridiculous to be confronted by this kind of person. Fortunately, I have never met anyone like that in here. However, as the saying goes, "there is no better way to stop evil speaking than self-cultivation," China has to win credit for herself; otherwise, those from other countries will look down upon us even if they do not say so.

We chatted until 8:40 p.m. when McDougall suggested going to the movies. As the movie was so bad, I did not stay at the small theater for more than half an hour. Back in my room, I wrote in my diary, practiced Tai-Chi and went to bed at about midnight.

April 27, 1946, Saturday

I went to the Chinese Delegation with Secretary Fang this morning. I showed to Gen. Zhu the "guest list for the Tribunal's banquet" which I was going to present to the judges. I discussed with him, asking him how many and who from the Delegation should be included, and whether there was anyone from the GHQ having special relations with or friendly feelings toward China who should be added to the list.

Gen. Zhu mentioned seven or eight names that should be included in the list. Back at the Tribunal's office, I sorted out the list of guests I proposed, and gave it to McDougall (who is now regarded as our "liaison officer"). As for the guests from the GHQ who should be invited, such as Supreme Commander MacArthur, Chief of Staff Qian, Mr. Keenan and so on, I completely followed Northcroft's list as it was all inclusive, with the only addition of four: Gen. Marquat (Director of the Scientific and Economic Group of the GHQ, Tokyo Air Defense Commander, and the recently resigned representative and acting chairman of the Allied Council for Japan), Col. Fellers (Secretary General of the Allied Council for Japan), Mr. Sutton and Col. Morrow of the IPS who had just come back from China. As for the Chinese Delegation, I only listed its head Gen. Zhu Gongliang, Chief Adviser Mr. Shen Jinding and Chief Liaison Officer Maj. Gen. Wang Danru. I had planned to include Dr. Li Jizhi and Mr. Yun Zhen, but did not do so as they would leave Japan in just a few days.

I did some routine work in the office, and had a cup of coffee with Higgins in the bar. He was still eager to travel to Shanghai and Peking after the delivery of the Indictment. Given the chaotic situation, soaring prices and difficult transportation in China, I could only listen and say nothing but beat around the bush.

I took a nap after lunch, and went to the Joint Staff Office to look at the dispatches from the Chinese Central News Agency over the past few days. Such dispatches are the only source in Tokyo of China's domestic news in detail, but what the Agency does is no more than taking down from China's radio broadcast a dozen pieces of news each day. I was talking with Danru when suddenly a telephone call came to the Joint Staff Office from the GHQ, saying that a Chinese aircraft had arrived at Atsugi Airport. This surprised and baffled us. Danru sent Col. Qian and Maj. Col. Luo to receive them at the airport.

I chatted with Danru after returning to the hotel, where Secretary Fang and Secretary Liu also joined us. After dinner, I watched a movie at the small theater, and then came back to my room to practice Tai-Chi and write in my diary. As it was Saturday, there was a dance party in the dining hall. At 10:00 p.m., the sound of the music rose up, and a waiter told me that there was a song and dance show. I went downstairs to see it. It was not the Japanese dance, but some Japanese girls imitating Western songs and dances, which they did not do well. Two singers, short and fat, were pretty disgusting with poor voice and facial expression. Not even as good as an ordinary song and dance troupe in China, how could they be invited to perform at the Imperial Hotel?

I received a call from Luo Jiyi after coming back to my room. It turned out that today's Chinese airplane brought here the third batch of the Delegation members, and Luo arrived in Tokyo by the same plane. I went to bed at about midnight after taking a shower.

April 28, 1946, Sunday

Gen. Wang and Secretary Fang came over early in the morning. We rode together to the place of the Chinese Delegation to visit those who arrived yesterday. Secretary Luo told me some domestic developments as well as his journey. He brought seven or eight letters for me. Apart from letters from my father, Boping and Wanru, there were also letters from Wu Shangying, Liu Jiefu, Jiang Xiangduo and Ren Jiafeng. I spent more than one hour reading the long letters written by my father and by Wanru, which contained several newspaper clippings, mainly reports on the Tokyo Tribunal, such as the arrival of the judges, the current status of the war criminals, and so on. The facts that I arrived in Tokyo on March 20 and that Gen. MacArthur invited us to lunch on April 12 were reported conspicuously by Central Daily News and Ta Kung Pao. After that, I chatted with Gen. Zhu and skimmed through some of the newspapers brought over by the newcomers from China, until it was after 12 noon before I realized it.

I went back to the hotel and had lunch. After taking a nap, I studied carefully the Rules of Procedure adopted by the Tribunal and several documents it had issued recently. At dusk, I went with Danru to see the house he was getting renovated. The house was requisitioned for him by the GHQ a few months ago. The environment was elegant, the garden vast and the interior magnificent. There were about a dozen rooms, more than enough for a small family.

After dinner, I went to the movies with Danru at the small theater downstairs. I practiced Tai-Chi at 11:00 p.m., and then went to bed. I read the long letters from my father and from Wanru twice again in the bed. Although they were just about some family chores and news on relatives and friends, I found them very interesting. An ancient poem says, "Letters from home are worth ten thousand pieces of gold," which I feel especially meaningful under the present circumstances.

April 29, 1946, Monday

Today was the day that witnessed the very first big event marking the official commencement of the Tribunal's operation, that is, submission of the Indictment to the Tribunal. It was scheduled for 10:30 a.m., and I, together with Secretary Fang, came to the courthouse at 9:30. After finishing several routine matters, I went to the conference room with McDougall and others, where we had a casual talk.

At 10:30, Chief Prosecutor Keenan, followed by the associate prosecutors from different countries, appeared in the conference room with the original of the Indictment in hand. The Chinese persecutor Xiang Mingsi was absent as he went back to China, while his secretary Liu Zijian filled in for him. The judges took their seats around the table, the Chief Prosecutor sat opposite to the President, and the associate prosecutors used the chairs by the window.

Chief Prosecutor Keenan made his statement to the judges, in which he briefly introduced the process of the preparation for prosecution and asked for permission to file the Indictment. President Webb granted his request and ordered the General Secretary to issue a receipt. The Chief Prosecutor was then invited to sit in on the judges' conference and give his opinion on fixing a date for the beginning of the court hearing, in other words, the date of the arraignment. On that day, the Tribunal would formally open, accept the prosecution, and ask each of the accused whether he would plead "guilty" or "not guilty." The arraignment is a special procedure in the common law system, while the civil law countries do not distinguish between indictment and arraignment.

Mr. Keenan indicated that the prosecution had made plenty of copies of the Indictment, which could be served to the accused by the Tribunal today; as their decision to plead not guilty or guilty was an easy and simple one to make, he deemed it sufficient to give the accused three or four days to consider. Based on this opinion, the Tribunal resolved to open the trial at 10:30 a.m. this Friday, when the prosecution would officially announce its Indictment, and the accused, in the presence of their lawyers, should respond to the charges by pleading not guilty or guilty.

After this decision was made, the Chief Prosecutor and the associate prosecutors from different country withdrew from the conference room, and the so-called "Return of Indictment" was finished, lasting for less than one hour. This was a ritual performed with judges "sitting in chamber," as opposed to that performed with judges "sitting in open court."

After the meeting, there came quite a few journalists and photographers, one of whom was Mr. Zhang Renzhong, the special correspondent of the Chinese Central News Agency in Tokyo, a vigorous and capable young man. He asked the photographer to take a photo for the two of us together, then followed me to my office and asked some questions. He was very pleased that my seating position was the second one among the judges, immediately to the left of the President. He said that there had been rumors about the judges' seating arrangement and that he was aware of the unavoidable overt contention and covert struggle surrounding this matter. He congratulated me for having been able to maintain our country's well-deserved international status, and said that he would telegram home to publicize it to our fellow countrymen. As I responded to him, I cannot take the credit because it all results from our Chinese people fighting in blood for eight years against the Japanese aggression. As long as our country spares no effort in peaceful construction, our international status will remain unchanged. But if we fail to live up to the expectations, our status in any international occasion, I am afraid, will suffer a disastrous decline.

I asked Secretary Fang to explain to him in detail the situation in the Tribunal and some ongoing steps taken in the past few days. Zhang left at noontime, afterwards I joined Higgins, Röling and others in the bar, and found Zaryanov also there. Everyone felt cheerful about the fact that the wheels of justice have start turning now.

Back in the hotel, Mr. Yun Zhen and Dr. Li Jizhi whom I invited to lunch had already been waiting in my room. Mr. Yun would in two days fly to the US to attend the conference on war reparations held by the Far Eastern Commission in Washington, DC. Dr. Li would go back to China the day after tomorrow since there was a lot of work awaiting him in the Academia Sinica and the National Museum.

The lunch was served in my room, and we were happily eating and talking. Time went so fast that it was 3:00 p.m. when we said goodbye to each other.

After taking a nap, I went to the Joint Staff Office to read the dispatches from the Chinese Central News Agency, and then brought Danru back to the hotel.

Miss. Wang, whom I came across a few days ago as the first Chinese young lady I had met in Japan, came to see Danru for some matters. Danru then asked me to join them for dinner in the dining hall. Afterwards we saw a color movie and found it jolly but rather empty in terms of the plot, which is generally true for most American movies.

After the guest left, I practiced Tai-Chi, took a shower and went to the bed at about midnight.

April 30, 1946, Tuesday

There was no judges' meeting today. It was cloudy and rainy. I did not show up in the courthouse but sent Secretary Fang to take Secretary Luo there, to show him around and to check, just in case that something would happen.

Staying in my room, I carefully studied the Rules of Procedure and dealt with some Tribunal affairs relating to the translation in court. Later, I caught up on my diary writing.

Secretary Fang made an appointment with Mr. Song Dehe (Norman Soong), a reporter from the Chinese Central News Agency, to have lunch with me at noontime in the hotel. Mr. Song is well known in China as a military correspondent who followed the Allied forces to land at the Pacific Islands and mainland Japan. He is also one of the pillar reporters of the Central News Agency, and I have read many of his news reports. A man in his early 30's, Song is fluent in English and acts dynamically and creatively. He told me that the Central News Agency had a high social status in Tokyo, which even went above and beyond the Associated Press or the United Press International, but it struggled a lot because of a staff shortage. After his assistant Mr. Zeng went back to China, said Song, he had to perform a one-man show (he himself had just returned from China as well). Song indeed has a clear insight about Japan's domestic situation, and had maintained a good relationship with the GHQ and the Japanese government. While admitting that Gen. MacArthur's increasingly lenient policy toward Japan is dangerous, he stays optimistic about the development of international situation in general. In his opinion, the US cannot and will never abandon China; neither does he feel pessimistic over the news that the negotiations between the KMT and the CPC have failed since President Chiang Kai-shek has finally rejected the CPC's claim on Northwest China (which claim was passed to the KMT via Gen. Marshall).

We had a very good talk until 2:00 p.m. After he left, I went straight to the courthouse to take part in the court-opening rehearsal.

The rehearsal today was attended by all the prosecutors (the Chinese prosecutor being represented by Adviser Shen Jinding of the Chinese Delegation) and the court staff, but it turned out to be a failure. The plan was to test the effect of translation, from English to Japanese and vise versa, as well as the speed and skills of the interpreters. However, President Webb kept proceeding in English, while the General Secretary and the Court Marshal dared not interrupt and stop him, so the intended test was not conducted at all. Webb was very much dissatisfied with it and decided to try it again tomorrow, without the presence of the other judges.

After the rehearsal, the judges gathered for about half an hour. Then I went back to my office and found that Mr. Shen, Secretary Luo and Secretary Fang were all waiting for me. I ordered coffee and talked with them for half an hour, after which I accompanied Mr. Shen back to the Chinese Delegation. I also got off the car and went in there to have a short chat with Gongliang.

Back to the hotel for dinner, my fellow judges and I talked quite a lot. We thought today's rehearsal ridiculous since it achieved nothing.

Danru asked me to go to the movies at 8:40 p.m. We walked out before the movie ended and talked in my room, mostly about the organizational and personnel issues of the Chinese Delegation. Danru complained a lot, but had quite some unique views as well. He has served as the liaison officer in MacArthur's headquarters for five years, starting back in the Philippines; he certainly has deeper insights on how to advance the communication and relationship between China and the US. After Danru left, I played Tai-Chi, wrote in my diary, and went to bed at almost 1:00 a.m.

May 1, 1946, Wednesday

I woke up in the morning and opened the newspapers, only to see the headlines that some Japanese mobs intended to assassinate Supreme Commander MacArthur on the Labor Day, with photos of the suspects printed. But reading the relevant articles, I found them short of details and rather empty. I suspect that this was published for some hidden purposes.

Although there was no judges' meeting today, I still went to the courthouse in the morning, since I would leave in the afternoon to spend the Labor Day break with Danru in Atami, for sightseeing and hot spring bathing. I did some routine work and chatted for a short while with my next-door neighbor McDougall.

Returning to the hotel, Mr. Song Dehe from the Chinese Central News Agency came to invite Secretary Fang and me to lunch. He said that he lived in a co-rented house with three American journalists; while we could have had some Chinese food there, the cook took leave today, giving him no choice but to take us to the Press Club.

We ate and talked to our heart' content in the dining hall of the Press Club, and ran into Mr. Zhang Renzhong and some American reporters. Journalists are always lively and active. The air exchanging system and even the waitresses here are different from the Imperial Hotel, which by comparison lacks youthful vigor.

I asked Mr. Song what he thought of the headlines on "assassinating Supreme Commander MacArthur." He seemed to agree that it served some hidden purposes, and answered my question by asking whether I had noticed that, in the newspapers, any mentioning of tomorrow's "parade" was always accompanied by the name "Communist Party." We said nothing but smiled at each other.

After a nap, Danru came at 3:00 p.m. We obtained some food as dinner from the hotel manager's office and started our trip to Atami by my car. There was a Japanese sharing ride with us, who commuted between his job in Tokyo and home in Atami every day. He was with us when we went to Atami last time and, for convenience's sake, we gave him a lift this time, too. He told us that his father was a merchant, and that he had been to Shanghai. He claimed that he was against the warlords' invasion of China even before the war, and that he wrote some articles to condemn the war. Only God knows whether what he said was true, and we did not take it seriously. We took him along because he was a native of Atami who might bring us some convenience and also make our ride less boring by talking about the scenery and historical sites in the region.

The journey took us about three hours and we arrived in Atami at dusk. The Sanno Hotel we stayed in, different from last time's Daikokuya, was in Western rather than Japanese style. The rooms were clean and tidy. Supervised and managed by the GHQ, the hotel was excellent in terms of sanitation and order. There was an old man among the attendants who had been to Europe and could speak English, so we felt convenient as he helped us translate when we needed something.

When our rooms were ready, we started to have dinner. At 8:00 p.m., the Japanese who rode with us brought us some side dishes prepared by his wife to relieve the effect of alcohol, and he also brought a phonograph from home. We therefore listened to music while drinking—I drank tea instead of wine—and it was after 9 o'clock before we realized it. I then wandered around the street for half an hour, took a bath in a hot spring (for which Atami is famous in the world), and went to bed before 11 o'clock as a result of the weary journey.

Today, we traveled through many small villages, noticing their houses, regardless of whether they were homes in the rural area or stores along the street, were all made of glasses and wood blocks, looking very much like pigeon cages or match boxes, without tall and thick walls and fences, or door bolts plus locks as we see in China. This shows that public security seems not to be a problem in Japan. But I wonder whether this is a scenario that has been in existence from ancient times, or one that came into being when Japan and its people became prosperous after the industrialization. It is a question worth probing into. Thinking of the dreadful picture of the Chinese countryside, I feel sad and terrified.

May 2, 1946, Thursday

Tomorrow will mark the grand opening of the International Military Tribunal for the Far East. Although we were still in the Labor Day break, I was concerned that there might be an impromptu judges' conference and therefore woke up before 6:00 a.m. Atami was renowned for its hot springs. I again took a bath in a small hot spring pool before leaving, and then headed for Tokyo with Danru by car after having just a quick breakfast. While looking sleepy, our driver drove steadily and fast. We arrived at the Imperial Hotel as early as before 9:30 in the morning.

Secretary Fang called to tell me that there would be no judges' meeting and only three or four judges were in the office. I then decided not to go to the Tribunal but to devote all my time to a thorough reading of the Indictment.

The Indictment is quite long; the English version that I read densely fills some forty large typewritten pages. But the main part covers only 14 pages while the rest are appendices.

There are totally 55 counts divided into three groups:

Group One: Crimes against peace (counts 1–36)
Group Two: Murder (counts 37–52)
Group Three: Conventional war crimes and crimes against humanity (counts 53–55)

Twenty-eight Japanese war criminals have been charged, most of them being top leaders with significant responsibilities in the various areas of politics, military, economy, culture and education. Their names are listed as follows in alphabetic order of their surnames in English.

1. Araki, Sadao;
2. Dohihara, Kenji;
3. Hashimoto, Kingoro;
4. Hata, Shunroku;
5. Hiranuma, Kiichiro;
6. Hirota, Koki;
7. Hoshino, Naoki;
8. Itagaki, Seishiro;
9. Kaya, Okinori;
10. Kido, Koichi;
11. Kimura, Heitaro;
12. Koiso, Kuniaki;
13. Matsui, Iwane;
14. Matsuoka, Yosuke;
15. Minami, Jiro;
16. Muto, Akira;
17. Nagano, Osami;
18. Oka, Takasumi;
19. Okawa, Shumei;
20. Oshima, Hiroshi;
21. Sato, Kenryo;
22. Shigemitsu, Mamoru;
23. Shimada, Shigetaro;
24. Shiratori, Toshio;
25. Suzuki, Teiichi;
26. Togo, Shigenori;
27. Tojo, Hideki;
28. Umezu, Yoshijiro.

I know most of the names of those twenty-eight accused, almost all of whom have brought catastrophe to China. Dohihara, in particular, is the most intricate and cunning one who stood out as an expert in tearing China apart and spent most of his life in afflicting and destroying China. The second one is Matsui, commander-in-chief of the troops which committed the Nanking Massacre, whose name will be engraved into the Chinese people's memory as a chief headsman. Those who served as military leaders in the invasion of China, like Itagaki, Koiso, Umezu and so on, are well known by the Chinese people. As for Matsuoka who attended the League of Nations Assembly after the Mukden Incident, Shigemitsu who lost a leg in Hongkou during the Songhu Battle, and Hirota who made up the Three Principles on the Sino-Japanese relations, their fate was closely connected with China in the past two or three decades and the Chinese people are quite clear of who they are.

The Indictment is so long that I finished reading only one-third of it before lunch. Then I took a nap and played Tai-Chi, before I resumed reading at 4:00 p.m. My anger grew with each page, and I finally finished reading the main text by 6:00. Danru came for a chat and, coincidentally, Xiang Mingsi had just returned from China in order to attend the big ceremony tomorrow. Over tea and some snacks, we had a joyful talk with one another.

Dr. Li Jizhi would go back to China by the chartered plane which was to fly to Shanghai the day after tomorrow. Given that I could be fully occupied by the Tribunal's opening tomorrow, I had to rush out some letters tonight so that Dr. Li could take them for mailing in China.

After dinner, I immersed myself into letter writing and finished eight of them, one of which was for the president of the Legislative Council, Mr. Sun Ke, to ask for another 3-month leave of absence, as the previously granted 3-month leave, starting from February 10, would expire on the 10th of this month. The other letters were written to my father, Boping, Uncle Yangchun, Qiuyuan, Yifei, Minheng, Jiefu (enclosing that to Wanru), Jichun and some friends at Fudan University. Each of these letters enclosed two newspaper clippings in English, covering the gist of the Indictment, the trial procedures, photos of the courtroom and the judges, and the individual pictures of the war criminals (whose names in Chinese were noted by Secretary Luo at my request). I could thus be very brief in my own writing as the enclosures would reveal exactly what I wanted to tell them.

In this way, I finished within two hours eight content-rich letters, with their envelopes written and stamps stuck. I felt quite satisfied and went to the bar for a cup of Coca Cola. I ran into President Webb there, and he said: "Tomorrow is our grand opening day; you may want to go to bed early tonight." We smiled at each other and said good night. I wrote in my diary, and eventually went to bed at 1:00 a.m. So be it!

When driving through Yokohama on our way back from Atami, we saw many labor groups on parade. They marched in good order, and the workers, both men and women, were tidily dressed and looked quite strong. I could say that there was no sign of malnutrition among the thousands of people. I wonder why Gen. MacArthur's GHQ was so considerate of the Japanese people for food scarcity, and why they made meticulous plans for them. Such a defeated country should really be regarded as "God's favored one." As compared to my victorious country in great difficulty and misery, I cannot but sigh for our inferiority.

Another thing worth noticing was that there were a lot of red flags in the Labor Day parade. I asked a Japanese intellectual about it, and he told me that it had not been like this in the past years. Red flags stand for revolution and even Communism. The world is moving toward the left as a general trend, which no one can stop.

May 3, 1946, Friday

Today was the very first day that the International Military Tribunal for the Far East started its performance, and also the first act of this historical drama in which I play a role as a guest performer.

I recalled the story of three months ago when I received the government's appointment in Chungking. As I lacked judicial experience and felt reluctant to leave my parents who were about to retire to my hometown, I submitted my resignation immediately on the day following my reception of the appointment order, which I returned to the Executive Council via the Ministry of Foreign Affairs. Only a few days later, President Sun of my Legislative Council wrote me a letter at the request of the Foreign Ministry, to talk me out of the resignation. President Sun himself also tried his best to persuade me into accepting this appointment. He said to me that it would really be a once-in-a-blue-moon opportunity, not only valuable and interesting but would also make you remembered in history. "Could you imagine half a year ago that we would feel pride and elation today?" said he, "What was it like this day of last year, when Dushan county and Duyun county were under attack and even people in Chungking were panic-stricken?" I responded to him that the rise and fall of a nation was unpredictable and all these changes seemed to us like a drama. President Sun said that the world was indeed a stage and history was but a series of dramas played on that stage. Since it was a drama, you'd better play a role in it.

And now I am truly playing a role in this drama, which is about to begin.

The Tribunal opening was scheduled for 10:30 a.m. and I went there at 9:30 to avoid any possible traffic jam and in case there would be an unscheduled judges' conference. I found nothing unusual along my way but when we were close to the former War Ministry Building, there were more people and cars than usual, and the security measures were stricter at the entrance. Entering the gate, I saw rows of vehicles on the square, among which a tightly closed ambulance-like bus was said to have carried twenty-six war crime suspects from Sugamo Prison and arrived at 8:30 this morning. The remaining two were escorted to Tokyo from Southeast Asia this morning.

I went to my own office as usual. McDougall arrived earlier than me and dropped by for a few minutes. Shortly after 10 o'clock, Gen. Zhu Gongliang came in with Secretary Luo (whom I sent to pick him up). After talking with Gen. Zhu briefly, I asked Secretary Luo to lead him to the VIP section. Then I put on my robe, went to the conference room and talked with my colleagues. Almost all nine of us had arrived. Also present there was Lord Wright, who made a special trip to Japan to observe our trial (he had observed the Nuremberg Trial, too). He is an elder man and is considered an authority on international law.

At the scheduled time of 10:30 a.m., the Court Marshal came in to report that the plane to transport Seishiro Itagaki and Heitaro Kimura from Siam had arrived at Atsugi Airport, and that the vehicle carrying the two prisoners was running at full speed toward Tokyo and should arrive soon.

We were delighted to hear this news and decided to instruct the Court Marshal to announce to the audience a 30-minute delay, lest we would have to repeat the "show" for those two prisoners on another day.

It was already 11:10 a.m., but there was no sign of their arrival. When calling the airport, we were told that they left the airport only twenty minutes ago, which meant that at least one more hour was needed for them to arrive at the courtroom. To avoid disappointing the audience, we decided to open the Tribunal right away but not to read out the Indictment until the court session resumed in the afternoon.

There was no question concerning the order of the judges' entry and seating—the President had advised us in writing earlier today. Apart from for the President leading in front, our line and seats followed the sequence of the US, China, the UK, the Soviet Union, Canada, France, the Netherlands, New Zealand, India and the Philippines. We filed in, where I walked between the judges from the US and the UK. When we approached the door, the Court Marshal loudly proclaimed "Silence!" and then "All rise!" as we entered the courtroom. We stepped onto the platform one after another and stood behind our big chairs until everyone was in the right position, and together we sat down. When all the judges took the bench, the Court

Marshal shouted: "Be seated!" Only then did the prosecutors, the staff and the spectators take their seats.

As the courtroom was big, the corridor long and the platform high, and especially because of the large number of judges wearing inconvenient long robes and moving slowly, the mere process of entry into the courtroom took nearly ten minutes. That was the tensest moment, when the flickering flashlights from everywhere made the courtroom like an open square bathed in the sun, and the cameras and cine-cameras were shooting non-stop.

Sir William Webb, the President, started to read his prepared opening speech, followed by a Japanese translation, as in accordance with the Charter, everything in this trial must be done bilingually.

When the President was making his opening speech, I took a careful look at the courtroom.

The seats in front of and below the judges' platform were for the General Secretary, the Registrar, the Clerk and the secretary of each judge. Secretary Fang sat on the third seat from the right.

The prosecutors were facing the judges and their secretaries. Mr. Keenan, the Chief Prosecutor, sat in middle of a rectangular table, around which were the associate prosecutors from China, the UK, the Soviet Union, Australia, Canada, France, New Zealand, India and the Philippines. There were two big tables on both sides of the prosecutors, one for the defense lawyers and the other for the recorders and translators. The amplifiers were located between the table for the prosecutors and that for the defense lawyers.

Behind the three large tables was the dock for the accused, which was a rectangular platform a few feet above the ground. All the twenty-six war criminals were sitting up straight in two rows. Under the strong light, the gleaming camera flash and people's close attention on us, I had no time to match all those defendants' faces with their pictures, which were arranged according to their seating positions and provided to each of the judges. The only ones who caught my eyes were Tojo sitting in the middle and Dohihara with a round face. Behind Tojo was Shumei Okawa, who pretended to have mental disorder and tried to commit harassment from time to time. The American military police wanted to stop him from doing so, and sometimes had to hold him from behind. Okawa had submitted a written application to have his mental and physical conditions examined. He was no doubt the one who acted most ridiculously and drew the highest attention, while all the others managed to keep a stern face and look calm, especially Tojo who sat still like a gypsum statue.

While not being able to recognize those twenty-six war criminals one by one, an endless resentment and sorrow welled up in my mind when facing this crowd. All these men were old hands in the invasion of China. They afflicted China for decades and butchered tens of millions of Chinese people. My resentment toward them reflects that of my fellow countrymen. The opportunity I can sit at the bench today to punish these culprits was built on the flesh and blood of millions and millions of my compatriots. I shall be vigilant! I shall be solemn!

There is a balcony to the right of the bench. The ground level was totally occupied by journalists and photographers, about 400–500 in total, with half from the Allied countries and half from Japan. They were definitely the busiest group today. The spectators' seats on the balcony were also divided equally between those for Allied nationals and those for Japanese. Doubtlessly, the balcony was packed with people, but remained in good order since access was only granted to those with tickets. Today's spectators were considered lucky or well connected to find their way into the courtroom. It was said that all the tickets were sold out a week ago.

There is another balcony to the left of the bench, with a smaller space that may hold 100–200 people. This is the VIP section. Today, all the guests sitting there were truly the most important officials in Tokyo from the Allied countries, especially the senior military officers of the US army, navy and air force. General Zhu Gongliang, taken care of by Secretary Luo, was the only Chinese guest there. He drew quite some attention as he was sitting next to Gen. Eichelberger, Commander of the US Eighth Army and the number one favorite officer of Gen. MacArthur. MacArthur himself did not show up; it was said that he went to welcome former President Hoover who came to investigate the food scarcity in the Far East.

After the opening speech by President Webb, Chief Prosecutor Keenan requested to introduce his associate prosecutors. Chinese prosecutor Xiang Mingsi was the first one that was introduced, and Lopez from the Philippines was the last.

Then, under the supervision of the Court Marshal Van Meter, the court reporters and the American and Japanese interpreters took their oaths.

When all those rituals were finished, the President adjourned the court until 2:30 p.m., when the other two defendants would have arrived and the Indictment would be formally read out.

The Court Marshal proclaimed "All rise!" and we filed out. After a short break in the conference room, we returned to the hotel for lunch.

I took a nap for about an hour and reached the Tribunal before 2:30 p.m. The opening process went the same as in the morning, and the courtroom was still crowded with spectators. I found two more defendants in the dock: Seishiro Itagaki and Heitaro Kimura, who were flown back to Tokyo from Siam by special airplane this morning. I knew very well the name of Itagaki who was a key person in the aggressive war against China. I would definitely keep a close watch on him.

Being on the first day of the trial, everything was new and novel to me. I was too busy to identify each of the accused but, when seeing them sitting in the dock, I could not hold my feeling of indignation as if the resentment and sorrow from all my fellow countrymen would burst out in my heart. Fortunately, this is just the beginning of the trial, and these arch war criminals will stand no chance of getting away from the stern punishment in the name of justice and fairness, now that they have been put in the hands of the law.

The agenda was very simple this afternoon: the Court Marshal Van Meter and the Deputy Clerk Dell in turn read out the Indictment. After each count was read, its interpretation followed. The interpretation between two languages caused inevitable inconvenience, which I hope could be minimized when the eight hundred sets of earphones being shipped from America would arrive here.

It took the court two hours to read only 22 counts, and the President announced court adjournment until 9:30 a.m. tomorrow. An accident happened at that moment—Okawa who acted crazy hit Tojo twice in the head while yelling "I'm going to kill Tojo," which made the courtroom burst into laughter.

We retired to the conference room and discussed the issue of Okawa over a cup of coffee. We all agreed to grant him permission and hold him on remand in Sugamo Prison, and in the meantime designate two doctors to check his mental and physical conditions in order to see whether he would be fit to stand trial.

We left hastily after the decision was made. The first toilsome day finally came to an end!

I was in a big hurry to sort out the letters and pack up the presents for Wanru, as the Chinese plane was set to return to Shanghai tomorrow.

I made my way to the Chinese Delegation by car at 7:30 p.m. and delivered my package to Dr. Li Jizhi in person. We talked for some ten minutes and bade farewell to each other. I rushed back to the hotel for dinner, which I did not finish until 9 o'clock. McDougall and others asked me to see a movie, but I left before it ended as I was very tired. Having followed my routine to play Tai-Chi and take a shower, I went to bed at about midnight.

Today is the day when the machine has truly been started. I hope everything from now on will develop rapidly with no more procrastination. I feel unspeakable elation when thinking of this.

May 4, 1946, Saturday

The Tribunal entered its second day of the trial. Upon getting up, I skimmed through *Stars and Stripes* and *Nippon Times*, both of which were full of reports on yesterday's trial opening and various photos of the judges, the defendants, the bailiffs, etc. The most conspicuous picture was a panorama of the courtroom that occupied half of the page, and the incident of Okawa hitting Tojo twice in the head became the most reported story.

The court session opened at 9:30 a.m. today. I arrived at the courthouse at 9 o'clock and talked to my colleagues for half an hour in the conference room.

The trial began exactly in the same way as yesterday and the spectators' enthusiasm remained so high that all the seats were packed. After we stepped onto the platform and sat down, the President instructed the Deputy Clerk to resume the Indictment-reading from Count 23. As usual, the reading was followed by translation paragraph by paragraph, which was unavoidably boring.

During the long process of Indictment-reading, I paid special attention to discerning the defendants' postures and facial expressions. I tried to identify each defendant by referring several times to his name, photo and seating position. Their names and countenances triggered a lot of my memories and detestation. In particular, Dohihara with a chubby cheek and sitting at the right end of the front row incurred the deepest hatred. He forced himself to stay composed and sometimes shuddered a lot with anxiety on his face. I could see Tojo sitting still just like yesterday, as though he was petrified. Sadao Araki, the 70-year-old man who had once trumpeted his ridiculous idea of conquering the Soviet Russia with a hundred thousand Shinai (bamboo swords), had silver mustache pretty long but not well trimmed as shown in his photo. This old man gave an obstinate look when he kept his eyes open and mouth muttering as if he was trying to say something. All the others, while having had great fame and prestige for a period of time, were sitting here right now and looking not more than any rank-and-file members of the public. No wonder an article in *Stars and Stripes* depicted them as being "not like a group of rulers of a once powerful empire." Indeed, those people had been totally deprived of the self-important and heroic air they once had—they became so ordinary that you could not even tell them from the common passengers you would see in any bus in Shanghai or Tokyo. The poorest guy was Yosuke Matsuoka who used to be very influential in the international arena. He had withdrawn from the League of Nations on behalf of Japan after the Mukden Incident and insulted China as being nothing but a geographical term. He had created the three-country Anti-Comintern Pact, established the Soviet-Japanese Neutrality Pact, and hugged and kissed Stalin at the Moscow Railway Station. Today, however, with a mustache as well as a beard, he looked pale and haggard. An English newspaper described that "he had a mustache and a beard," but they were in a mess without any combing and trimming. The next poor-looking one was Iwane Matsui, the principal offender in the Nanking Massacre, who was now sitting there just as meek as a sheep. And according to the newspapers, this general who used to commit mass murder looked now very much like a bank clerk who lost his job or failed to get paid for long. What a proper description it was! The image of Matsui reminded me of a character—Mr. Huang Xingsan, a mediocre office employee in the Chinese drama *Sunrise*.

There was not much difference in appearance between those defendants and us Chinese. By nature, China and Japan should have co-existed and achieved common prosperity, given that the two peoples share the same origin and use similar characters in our languages. However, those war wagers, as well as their predecessors, persisted in advocating the absurd theory of Japan supremacy to perplex their countrymen, which made them so arrogant and ignorant that they dreamed of conquering China, then East Asia, and finally the whole world. It was exactly those men sitting in the dock, who had never for a moment thought of doing the right thing and had always acted beyond their reach, dragged Japan into such an unprecedented havoc. They were not only the enemies of China and the world, but also the enemies of the Japanese people. Seeing the awkward expression on their faces, I felt at once anger of our nation, and sadness for the Japanese people belonging to the same race as us. I wish that, by taking part in this historical trial, I could contribute to the establishment of a new principle under which people from all different nations would respect and understand each other, and co-exist and achieve common prosperity together.

At 10:30 a.m., President announced a 15-minute recess, during which we went to the conference room for a cup of coffee.

When we returned to the courtroom at 10:45, Matsuoka's lawyer requested to excuse him from the hearing because of his poor physical condition. Webb asked the lawyer whether there was a danger for Matsuoka to pass out right away, and the lawyer answered "Yes!" However, Webb did not grant the permission but said that this issue would be decided by the judges' conference at the next break.

During the reading and translation of the Indictment, apart from observing the defendants, I was also trying to figure out how many counts were related to China. It turns out that, out of the 55 counts, 12 are completely on China and three are closely connected with China. Since we do not have a lot of evidence and supporting materials, I wonder whether the IPS will be able to prove all of those counts. I felt somewhat worried when thinking of this.

At about 11:30 a.m., the reading in both English and Chinese of the Indictment with 55 counts finally came to an end. However, this was but the main text of the Indictment, which constituted only one-third of the total, while the Appendices made up the remaining two thirds.

By then, a feeling of impatience and weariness pervaded the courtroom. The President asked the defense lawyers whether they would agree to waive the reading of the Appendices. The lawyers asked for a 10-minute recess for discussion, after which they responded with an affirmative answer. It was really a great relief for everyone, as otherwise at least another six or seven hours would be required to finish reading the rest of the Indictment in both languages.

Before 12 noon, President Webb adjourned the court, which would be resumed at 9:30 a.m. on Monday.

After leaving the courtroom, we had a chat in the bar, and then I returned to the hotel for lunch. These two days of work made me tense and tired, so my nap lasted until after 4:00 p.m.

I went for a ride for half an hour to breathe some fresh air, and then stopped by at the Joint Staff Office to look at the news dispatches from China. I learned that former President Hoover was going to China to investigate the food scarcity; Gen. Marshall was still busy mediating the conflict between the KMT and the CPC for a peaceful solution in China; the government announced postponement of the National Assembly, but made May 5 the day of celebration for the returning of China's capital to Nanking.

Shortly after returning to the hotel, I received a phone call from Gen. Gongliang inviting me to join them for dinner as soon as possible at Tianhua Mansion, a Chinese restaurant. When I arrived at 7 o'clock, I found that, apart from my friends Mingsi, Danru and Gongliang himself, there was a Col. Band, an American transportation commander, and two of his companions, Miss Shi and Miss Qi (medical doctor), who had just arrived in Japan.

We were still in high spirits after dinner, so all except Mingsi decided to go dancing in the Imperial Hotel. It was really for the first time after the war that some Chinese ladies came to dance at the Imperial Hotel, and naturally they attracted high attention. At 10:00 p.m., the Japanese song and dance troupe performed Western music and dance, which I found improved from their show last week. I had to say that the Japanese were good at imitating but often failed to seize the essence. The dancing party ended at midnight and people faded away. I returned to my room, took a shower, and finally finished this day at about 1:00 a.m. The past two days were truly novel and exciting.

May 5, 1946, Sunday

I got my mind so tensed up in the past two days that I decided to take a complete rest over this weekend. When Wallace came to ask about my schedule, I told him decisively, "I'm not going out today. You may go anywhere you want and enjoy yourself." Without any car waiting for me, I felt at ease and put away all possible plans.

Except for a short visit from Danru, I spent the whole morning making up for the missing parts of my diary. After lunch I had a nap and played Tai-Chi. (Recently I often took the exercise after a nap in the afternoon, which I think is healthier than doing it before going to bed at night. But sometimes there is not enough time or I may forget it, not like in the still of night, when I can easily remember this routine.)

I then spent two more hours continuing with my diary, until 5:00 p.m. when Gen. Gongliang came with the two young ladies whom I met at dinner yesterday evening. It turned out that they live in Yokohama and came to Tokyo for shopping. Gen. Zhu said that, when they heard that I was the only honored guest from China staying at the Imperial Hotel, they decided that they had to drop by for a visit. I ordered some tea and snacks, whisky and coca cola to serve my visitors. They left for Yokohama at 7 o'clock.

I had dinner at the reserved table for the judges. My colleagues and I felt quite delighted when exchanging our views on the development of the past two days, because the "machine" had already been started and was operating properly.

McDougall and Röling insisted on going to see a movie with me. The movie was rather baffling, and the occasional breakdown of the projector made me sneak out and go back to my room. After reading some newspapers and magazines, I went to sleep at 10:30, which was the earliest time ever since I came to Toyko. It would be the arraignment of the war criminals tomorrow, and probably another gripping act would be performed then.

May 6, 1946, Monday

Today was another stressful day. The trial opened at 9:30 a.m. The spectators' seats were still packed, but the VIP section was less crowded than the first two days. Gen. Zhu did not show up because he had to attend the military parade for former President Hoover.

The session started by the Chief Prosecutor introducing to the bench Mr. Menon, the Indian associate prosecutor who had just arrived in Tokyo. Then Dr. Kiyose, counsel for Tojo and representative of all the defense lawyers, introduced all the counsel respectively employed by the defendants. Those defense counsel looked ordinary, but were said to be among the best lawyers in Tokyo, including the head of the law school of Tokyo Imperial University and the president of Meiji University.

Kiyose seemed around 60 years old and of medium build among the Japanese. With his gray hair and beard and somewhat slovenly appearance, he looked like an old pedant. He always talked with a smile to show a humble and amicable temper. If his voice was not powerful, his words certainly were, after translated by a young man with excellent English. Kiyose was in the center of attention today.

He requested to speak and indicated that he wanted to challenge the judges on the bench and raise an objection to the scope of jurisdiction of the Tribunal.

Both the judges and the spectators felt some tension. Kiyose, on the other hand, took his time to raise four reasons why it was not proper for Sir William Webb to act as the President and a judge of the Tribunal. He did not substantiate his claim but only pointed out that Webb had served as chairman of the Australian War Crimes Commission and signed on an investigation report concerning the Japanese atrocities in New Guinea—which was a true fact. Hearing this, Webb felt quite bothered, and Keenan made one or two comments, but Kiyose never changed his mind.

Webb stated that, as the matter concerned him personally, it was necessary to make a decision at a judges' conference, in which he would not participate. He promised to have the result reported in court, and then announced a 15-minute recess.

All the eight of us (excluding Webb) retired to the conference room, and everyone was nervous, especially since Kiyose seemed to have said that he would challenge and object to each judge.

It was a heated discussion and all of us expressed our opinions. But I cannot publish or disclose the statements at the meeting of any judges except for those by myself, as otherwise it would violate the oath we took.

Surrounded by an air of tension, we reached a conclusion that, in accordance with Article 2 of the Tribunal's Charter, the members of the Tribunal were appointed by the SCAP based on the recommendation of their respective countries; that being the case, the judges were not authorized to dismiss or withdraw the appointment of any one of us from the Tribunal. After the decision was made, we invited Webb in and informed him about it.

It was about twenty minutes after the beginning of the recess that the court session resumed again. Sir William Webb was still presiding over it, while the spectators were wriggling and whispering with a sense of expectancy.

Before Webb started to speak, we recommended Northcroft to report briefly on the process and result of our discussion. After that, the session went back on track.

Then came today's most important program: each accused was to plead "guilty" or "not guilty" to the charges listed in the Indictment.

Sadao Araki was the first one to be called, because his surname starts with "A." This defiant old man seemed resentful and mumbled and sputtered quite a lot. I gave Webb a signal to interfere, and he cut Araki short and ordered him to plead guilty or not guilty instead of giving a speech. Without any patience, Araki said: "I have lived for 70 years and have never committed any crimes against peace or any other atrocities as charged."

The defendants after Araki stated in turn that they pleaded not guilty. Some of them, especially Akira Muto, former Chief of Staff of Tomoyuki Yamashita, answered with anger as if they had been giving orders on the troop training ground.

Yosuke Matsuoka was more Westernized after all. Although he was so sick that he looked on the point of dying, he answered in English which was not so fluent: "Not guilty to all and every count."

Being the 26th defendant to be called, Tojo attracted most of the attention, with many cameras pointing at him when he stood up. He said in a calm and loud voice: "On all counts, I plead not guilty."

The twenty-eight defendants, with the only exception of Okawa who was absent and suspended from entering a plea, made their statements one after another. The bench then asked both parties, the prosecution and the defense, about the date to actually start hearing the evidence, on which they argued a lot. Finally, after consulting with us, the President formally announced that the court was to reopen on May 13, next Monday, to argue and rule on the issue of jurisdiction; and on June 3, i.e., four weeks from today, to officially start the court hearing and admitting evidence. Then the session came to an end and the court would resume at 9:30 a.m. on Monday next week.

Back in the hotel, I found Zhang Renzhong, the special correspondent of the Chinese Central News Agency in Tokyo, waiting for me here. We had lunch together and talked a lot about some domestic affairs, the Japanese political trends, and today's court session.

When Zhang left, I took a nap for about two hours and played Tai-Chi afterwards. Around 5 o'clock, I went to the Chinese Delegation to read the dispatches from the Chinese Central News Agency and some old newspapers. Gen. Zhu was very pleased, because the GHQ had prohibited Ichiro Hatoyama, the man opposed by the Chinese Delegation, from creating a cabinet. Therefore, Hatoyama had lost what he wanted on the verge of success, and he might even be listed as a war criminal.

As May 10 would be the last day of my 3-month leave of absence, I drafted a telegraph before I left the Chinese Delegation, asking the

Legislative Council for an extension, which I entrusted Gongliang to send to Nanking with their own telegraph transmitter.

Gongliang joined me for dinner at the Imperial Hotel, after which we went to the Pyle Theater and saw some acrobatic shows and a movie. There were still only the two of us in the "generals' box."

He left at 11:00 p.m., and I took a shower and went to bed.

May 7, 1946, Tuesday

I went to the courthouse in the morning and dealt with some daily routines. McDougall came and chatted with me for a while. Few of my colleagues had come in today, and I guessed it was because of yesterday's strenuous work. The American judge Higgins came to my office and, once again, talked about his long-desired trip to Shanghai. I told him that I would definitely go with him if there was a chartered plane available for us. "Let's make it happen," said he, who planned to work on it this afternoon.

I returned to the hotel for lunch, then took a nap and played Tai-Chi. Danru came at 5:00 p.m., and we had dinner together.

After dinner, I read carefully the newspapers of the past few days, to see how the press from different countries reacted to and commented on our accepting and hearing the cases. Generally speaking, the Japanese papers expressed satisfaction, since they wanted to shirk the responsibility and shift the blame onto those major war criminals. The Americans had quite divided opinions. Some thought that the number of the accused was too small and many of the prime culprits had escaped punishment. One newspaper, probably *Washington Sun*, said directly that the Emperor of Japan as the number one war criminal should not be allowed to go scot-free. The press from the dominions of the UK held the same opinion (Australia and New Zealand had long been insisting that the Emperor should be listed as a war criminal). While the press of the Soviet Union barely talked about the Tribunal, there was one newspaper advocated passionately that the Emperor should be put on trial. In my view, although for political reasons, the Emperor luckily escaped prosecution this time, such issue might unavoidably be brought up again one day, at least there is a possibility that he could be summoned to testify in court. This, of course, is but my personal perception and conjecture.

I finished reading many newspapers and clipped some articles, until it was after 11 o'clock before I realized it. I did not stop but rushed to write down what happened in the past two days into my diary, and finally went to bed at about 1:00 a.m.

May 8, 1946, Wednesday

Opening the newspapers when I got up, I found the news about China still occupying an outstanding position, mostly negative, though. While the government had successfully moved the capital back to Nanking, there was no sign of resolving the problems between the KMT and the CPC, and Gen. Marshall seemed at the end of his wits, too. According to Gongliang, former President Hoover had a discussion with Gen. MacArthur for quite a few hours when he came to Tokyo this time, expressing a pessimistic view on the China issues. No wonder when the journalists asked Hoover about China, he held his tongue and said nothing except that China was suffering miserably from natural disasters.

I had read before Gen. MacArthur's Japan management report for April, which said that Japan had been progressing toward a true democracy. Glorifying as it may, no one can deny that Gen. MacArthur's favorable policies have given Japan great economic advantage and have enabled it to gradually step onto the road to revival. In comparison with the current situation in China, one of the victorious nations, how can we not feel anxious and ashamed?

After breakfast, I reviewed the Chinese version of the Rules of Procedure translated by Secretary Fang and made a few revisions. I went to the office with it at 10:30 a.m., and asked Secretary Luo to transcribe the Chinese translation with his traditional brush pen.

Higgins called in when I was handling some routine work. He asked me to see him in his office so that we could discuss our planned trip to China during the court adjournment which would start after next Monday's session and last for about three weeks. His secretary Miss Ferros was desperately eager to go with us since her cousin was in Shanghai. We made a lot of phone calls to inquire about transportation and contacts, and the conclusion of all those discussions was that we would definitely need a chartered plane to make the trip. Regarding a possible detour to Peking, limited time for our stay in China (two weeks) as well as numerous turmoils there would make the matter of transportation very difficult. I said to Higgins: "I do not even know whether my wife has found her way to Shanghai from Chungking yet (I guess she should arrive on the 14th or 15th of this month, but I cannot say it for sure); if the GHQ provides us with an airplane, I promise to go back to China with you and play my role as a host." When we said goodbye, we wished each other good luck in finding a special plane.

I came back to the Imperial Hotel for lunch. Right after I woke up from a nap, Secretary Fang called from the office, saying that through Mr. Higgins's efforts, a chartered plane had tentatively designated for us; Higgins would discuss with me in details this evening or tomorrow morning. This made me feel surprisingly happy! Indeed, I will actually have a chance to go back to China within a few days!

From 5 to 7 o'clock in the afternoon, I studied the defense's motion on the jurisdiction of the Tribunal, for it would serve as the basis of the debate next Monday. There are four main points in the opinion, of which the most important two are as follows:

1. The Charter of the Tribunal provides for the punishment against waging of aggressive wars and breach of peace and humanity, which provision violates the Potsdam Declaration (the latter only mentioning that "stern justice shall be meted out to all war criminals"), and therefore constitutes ultra vires beyond its authorized scope.
2. A few counts in the Indictment are old stories having nothing to do with the recent war. In addition, Japan and the Soviet Union signed an agreement for peaceful resolution of their conflicts, and subsequently established the Soviet-Japanese Neutrality Pact, thus the two countries were not in a state of war at the time of the conflicts. To mention those old stories is not only unreasonable but can also be considered against the principle of non-retroactivity of law.

Those two points make some sense in terms of legal theories. The first point is relatively easy to deal with, while the second one seems much more complicated, and the fact that it concerns the Soviet Union alone makes it more subtle and tricky. After all, there must be a drastic debate next Monday, and our decision then can bear historic significance in legal history. I have to look deeper into those two points in advance.

After dinner, I read some newspapers and a book, and wrote in my diary. However, the planned returning trip to my motherland kept lingering in my mind. I made three phone calls to Higgins' room but there was no answer. By 11:30 p.m., this old gentleman still had not returned to his room. Perhaps he was also too excited, or perhaps he was still working on the airplane arrangements. Never mind, I played Tai-Chi, took a shower, and went to bed at almost 1:00 a.m.

May 9, 1946, Thursday

Shortly after getting up, I received a phone call from Higgins, who said that the difficulties in obtaining a chartered plane had basically been resolved with only some paperwork for us to go through. He asked me to meet with him at the office at 10:00 a.m. to discuss all the details. I answered him happily and expressed my admiration for his enthusiasm and efficiency.

At 10 o'clock we met in my office. General Secretary Walbridge asked us to fill in a form to explain the reasons why we would travel to China, which Higgins and I both signed. The three of us then discussed some of our traveling programs at length; Secretary Fang, a native of Shanghai, joined our conversation. We spent a pleasant time talking and Higgins even called himself an "admirer of China." It was said that apart from Higgins and myself, Secretaries Fang and Hua, and a crew of five members, there would also be Lt. Colbert who would act as our military aide. Everything has now been properly arranged and the only thing we are waiting for is the approval from the GHQ.

I went straight to the Chinese Delegation after leaving the office, because Mingsi called and asked me to meet him there. I had a long discussion with Gongliang and Mingsi about the two counts containing the words "Mongolian People's Republic" in the Indictment.

When we finished the discussion, Gongliang asked me to stay for lunch to try the two Chinese dishes recently added to their menu. Then I went back to the hotel and took a nap. After that, I practiced Tai-Chi and read some newspapers. The attendant sent in a document proposing the establishment of an "International Defense Section," which was submitted to Gen. MacArthur by Capt. Coleman (who wanted to amend the Charter for this purpose). I read it carefully and found it quite inappropriate.

After dinner, I talked with Webb about it. He felt the same way as I did, with even greater indignation. He said that he was going to discuss on how to deal with it at the judges' conference tomorrow.

Higgins had been looking forward to the trip to China. He came to talk with me for quite long, then we went to see a movie together, and afterwards we talked again in the bar. Finding him too excited, I reminded him not to hold his expectations too high, just in case the reality would disappoint him. He said in return that he would never be disappointed no matter what should happen on this trip.

We left each other at 11:00 p.m. I returned to my room, wrote in my diary, and went to bed around midnight.

May 10, 1946, Friday

Col. Hanney, Deputy General Secretary of the Tribunal, called early in the morning to tell me that there would be an ad hoc judges' conference at 10:00 a.m. I arrived at the courthouse at 9:30, and ran into the General Secretary at the entrance. He told me that the application for a chartered plane to China had been proved by the GHQ and a telegraph had already been sent to China. I was very pleased to hear this news. It is really amazing how the Americans handle things accurately and efficiently!

The 10 o'clock meeting focused completely on the submission to the GHQ by Mr. Coleman regarding amendment to the Charter by adding an "International Defense Section." We considered this request not only unnecessary but also highly absurd, because it was the defendants' own business to defend themselves; should the GHQ set up a special section and assign a "Chief Counsel of Defense," it would definitely be against the principle of fair trial as well as the common sense.

During the discussion, all my colleagues had consensus with a firm and resolute attitude. We decided to require Coleman to voluntarily withdraw his submission by 3:00 p.m. today, or we would make a direct and serious representation to Gen. MacArthur.

I returned to the hotel after the meeting. Shortly afterwards, Mr. Song Dehe came to invite me to lunch at his apartment, as he had prepared some Chinese dishes for me to try. We went together to his apartment, where he lives with four friendly American journalists. Song knows Japan very well and gets along with the American journalists like family members; that's probably why he is quite influential and resourceful in Tokyo. After lunch, we talked for another hour or so. According to his observation, there was still a possibility for the Emperor to be listed as a war criminal or summoned to appear in court as a witness; if so, said he, the Emperor would have to abdicate first. Our conversation covered a wide range of international and domestic affairs. At 2:30 p.m., I returned to the hotel, and went to the courthouse with Secretary Fang at 3 o'clock for a judges' conference.

President Webb informed us at the meeting that Coleman had withdrawn his submission but wished to come to this meeting in order to explain why he had appealed to the GHQ for the establishment of an International Defense Section. We granted his request, but he failed to explain it clearly despite his repetitive arguments. After he left the meeting, we discussed and drew a conclusion that not only was it unnecessary to set up an International Defense Section, but moreover, it made no sense at all if a "Chief Counsel of Defense" was to be appointed by the GHQ or the Tribunal. It should be decided by the defendants themselves, who should be given the freedom of choice. As for Mr. Coleman, he was no more than a petty administrator in charge of liaison with the defendants' lawyers, and it was not appropriate to call him "Chief Counsel of Defense." I spoke several times to make myself clear that such title had to be changed, and all my colleagues agreed with me. Finally, we instructed the General Secretary to arrange for the removal of Coleman's title as Chief Counsel of Defense, in order to avoid any possible misunderstanding. That marked the end of the side story started by Coleman.

After the meeting, I went back to the hotel to rest and read some newspapers. Secretary Luo and Gen. Wang came for a chat. Secretary Luo and I then went to Ginza to buy some gifts since I might go back to China soon. However, it was rather late and most of the stores were closed, so we ended up returning with empty hands.

After dinner, I had a long talk with Northcroft, Röling, McDougall and Bernard. They expressed surprise and admiration toward my firm attitude shown at the judges' conference. Indeed, I tend to ignore the trivialities but will never make a compromise on major issues. When something happens, I either stay out of it or, if I believe I should interfere, will do so with great persistence until a conclusion is reached, whether I win or lose.

At 8:40, McDougall asked me to go to the movies, but I stayed in the theater only for less than one hour. Then I carefully reviewed the Chinese version of the Charter translated by Secretary Fang until 11 o'clock. After practicing Tai-Chi and writing in my diary, I went to bed at around 1:00 a.m.

May 11, 1946, Saturday

I met with secretaries Fang and Luo at 9 o'clock in the morning. Luo gave me the transcribed Chinese translation of the Rules of Procedure. After discussion with Secretary Fang on the translation of the Charter, I made slight revisions and gave it to Secretary Luo to transcribe.

I asked Secretary Fang to go to the office and see if there was anything important, while I, accompanied by Secretary Luo, went to the stores at Kanda and Ginza. I bought some small gifts at Mitsukoshi and some dried seafood from a Chinese restaurant named Huifang Mansion for my families and friends. I was disappointed by the limited variety of products and the high prices, so I bought only a few items of local specialties, just to embellish my upcoming trip.

When I was back at the hotel, there was a note left by Mr. Zhang Renzhong of the Chinese Central News Agency, telling me that he had dropped by. Higgins asked me to have lunch together, as he was thrilled about the trip to China. It was only natural for the others to be envious, and one could not blame them for that.

I played Tai-Chi and read some newspapers after a nap. Shortly after, Danru and Mingsi stopped by and had a talk with me.

I had dinner with the other judges, as it would be inappropriate for me to do so with Mingsi. As the guests of Patrick and Northcroft, three officers from Hong Kong joined us in the dinner; they came to visit Tokyo with a British warship which would leave in two days.

I went back to my room after dinner and made some press clippings of the major news in the recent newspapers. At 10:00 p.m., I went to watch a show in the dining hall with Northcroft. The Japanese performers were imitating Western songs and dances, but far from perfection, and their unshapeliness made the show even less attracting.

I finished writing in my diary in my room and went to bed at about 12:30 a.m.

May 12, 1946, Sunday

I found on the newspapers some reports about the press conference given by Admiral Bruce Fraser, Commander of the British Pacific Fleet, who said that the Chinese people were all willing to have Hong Kong remaining under the British administration. Mr. Zhang Renzhong of the Chinese Central News Agency immediately stood up to argue with him, which should be considered brave and honorable, and should to a certain extent correct such irresponsible nonsense of those imperialists advocating "White Supremacy."

I went to the Chinese Delegation at 9:00 a.m. As it was Sunday and the delegates were not as occupied, I had a chance to meet with everyone there. At around 10 o'clock, I went back to the hotel, sorted out a few documents and found for Zhang Renzhong some materials on the Tribunal's trial proceedings. Gongliang called to invite me to try their new Chinese dishes, so I had lunch at the Delegation, but was not much impressed by their food. After taking a nap between 3 and 4 o'clock, I was told by both Danru and Col. Huff that Gen. Sun Liren [or as Sun Li-jen], Commander of the New First Army and a warrior who had fought meritoriously in the Burma Campaign, arrived in Tokyo and stayed in my hotel at Room 10 on the first floor. When I was about to go downstairs to pay him a visit, he came to my room together with Danru and Adjutant Zeng. I had some refreshments served and we had a good conversation. It was exactly two decades ago that Gen. Sun and I met each other, in the summer of 1926 when he was studying at Virginia Military Institute (V.M.I.), and Uncle Yangchun and I went to see him. Since then we pursued our separate courses and had no chance to see each other again. A lifetime seemed to have passed. This meeting certainly brought back a lot of memories and allowed us to catch up on each other's news, which made all sorts of feelings well up in our minds.

At 7:00 p.m., Gongliang invited Gen. Sun to a Chinese dinner at Jinghua Restaurant. I was naturally asked to join them, and so were Jinding, Mingsi, Danru and Gechuan. The dishes were so rich and tasteful that I considered this meal the very best one since my arrival in Tokyo. We talked while eating, covering a wide range of topics freely and unrestrictedly. It was 10 o'clock before we realized it.

I played Tai-Chi and wrote in my diary after returning to the hotel. Tomorrow's court session must be rather intense. I wanted to go to bed early but was too full to fall asleep. It was about 1:00 a.m. when I finally went to bed.

The frequent visits of various top leaders during the past few days made Tokyo busier than ever. After former President Hoover left, here came Gen. Eisenhower, who presided over a military parade this morning (in which Gongliang participated). In addition, Fraser, Commander of the British Pacific Fleet, and Pauley, Chairman of the US Committee on Japanese War Reparations, were also in Tokyo. It is a shame that our country is haunted by civil war and does not live up to the expectations of international community; otherwise this visit of Gen. Sun Liren, who is known to the world by his tremendous success in the battles against Japan in India and Burma, would definitely make a hit. At this point, I am in great sorrow seeing the decline of China's international status, and I am on the verge of throwing down my pen and breathing a deep sigh of sadness.

May 13, 1946, Monday

The court session opened at 9:30 a.m. The spectators, mostly Japanese, were very active, probably because they believed that the defendants' motion on the Tribunal's jurisdiction would make a big difference. Gen. Sun came to the courtroom and took a seat at the VIP section. I sent Secretary Luo to take care of him. His adjutant Mr. Zeng as well as Danru were also present.

First of all, the defense's representative Ichiro Kiyose elaborated on the written petition he submitted to the Tribunal. The old man delivered his speech in a slow and repetitive manner, and it lasted for one and a half hours including the time for translation. He talked a lot but we found nothing new from his written statement. He made a good deal of quotations, the purpose of which was nothing but to say that punishment on waging aggressive wars and crimes against peace and humanity under the Charter went beyond the scope of the Potsdam Declaration and was not permitted by the conditions of Japan's Instrument of Surrender. Kiyose thought that Japan's surrender was conditional, which in my opinion did not hold water at all.

The President announced a 10-minute recess. After the session resumed, Chief Prosecutor Keenan began to make a counter-argument by reading a prepared transcript. In less than ten minutes, Webb interrupted and asked him whether it was really necessary to use all those rhetorical phrases. Keenan became angry, replied sharply and resumed his reading. When Keenan was quoting some sentences from Stalin and Roosevelt, Webb cut him short again and said that his speech was too inflammatory. The rage-fueled Keenan retorted in response and, although he was able to finish his statement, he felt losing face. I signaled several times to stop Webb from interfering, as I felt he was swayed by personal feelings and was acting on impulse. Webb might have a problem with Keenan but it was not appropriate to hit back at him in court.

The court session stopped at noontime and would re-open at 1:30 p.m. In a great hurry, I went back to the hotel for lunch, took a 10-minute doze, and left for the courthouse together with Secretary Fang.

The time of 1:30 p.m. did not work well, especially for me. But the courtroom was still fully packed with spectators.

Keenan then introduced Comyns-Carr, the British associate prosecutor, to argue another aspect. Comyns-Carr read out his statement, as if it were an academic thesis, in some forty or fifty minutes. The statement was relatively rich and specific in terms of argumentative materials. While Keenan was delivering a speech to the whole world, Comyns-Carr was making a statement to the bench for the defense and justification of the Charter. It was a pity that Comyns-Carr was not very skillful in reading aloud, and the British accent was annoying, at least to me (since I was experiencing a strong feeling of resistance against Britain these days).

After a 10-minute recess, there came the Japanese translation of Comyns-Carr's statement. I put on my sunglasses and almost started to doze off. After that, Kiyose again gave his refutation without any new supporting ideas. Webb did not stop or interrupt him, except that he laughed at Kiyose for not knowing the difference between a conditional and unconditional surrender.

When Kiyose tried to quote from President Truman's speech in January of this year, Keenan could not put up with it anymore, so he protested to the bench. However, Webb seemed to hold strong prejudices against Keenan. Without inquiring the reason why Keenan was protesting, Webb asked Keenan in return why it was all right for him to refer to President Roosevelt but inappropriate for Kiyose to quote from President Truman. Keenan's red face and red nose turned into purple. He responded, with great anger, that he had quoted speeches delivered before the Potsdam Declaration, which could help explain people's understanding of war criminals at the Potsdam Conference. He further contended that the speech given by President Truman in January of this year had nothing to do with the topic of our debate, and that he was not trying to differentiate or discriminate any speaker. At this point Webb knew that his reasoning was weak, so he deliberately asked Higgins and me for advice on whether to accept Keenan's protest. Since both Higgins and I firmly supported its acceptance, Webb had to stop Kiyose's speech.

Such a tense situation, plus the heating and my heavy clothes made me dizzy. Fortunately the court was soon adjourned.

I returned to the hotel, had some tea and snacks, and took a nap. Later, I went to the store to buy something as gifts for my forthcoming trip to China.

When I had dinner at our "judges' table," I openly expressed to Northcroft, Röling, McDougall and Bernard my dissatisfaction with Webb's attitude today.

After dinner, Gongliang came and we went to Gen. Sun Liren's room for a talk. At 9:00 p.m., I returned to my room to write a couple of letters, which I asked Liren to take with him to China. I wrote in my diary before going to bed.

[After the above entry, there is a note in the original diary, reading: "From May 14 onwards, see another notebook." However, such "other notebook" has never been found. —Editor's note]

The manufacturer's authorised representative in the EU is Springer Nature Customer Service Centre GmbH, Europaplatz 3, 69115 Heidelberg, Germany. If you have any concerns regarding our products, please contact ProductSafety@springernature.com

Printed and bound by CPI Group (UK) Ltd, Croydon, CR0 4YY
25/09/2026
02222897-0015